Monsters & Magical Sticks

Monsters & Magical Sticks

There's No Such Thing As Hypnosis?

by

Steven Heller, Ph.D. & Terry Lee Steele

NEW FALCON PUBLICATIONS
TEMPE, ARIZONA, U.S.A.

International Standard Book Number: 1-56184-026-2
Library of Congress Catalog Card Number: 87-80595

First Edition 1987
Second Printing 1991
Third Printing 2001
Fourth Printing 2004
Fifth Printing 2005
Sixth Printing 2006

Cover by Amanda Fisher

The paper used in this publication meets the minimum requirements of the American National Standard for Permanence of Paper for Printed Library Materials Z39.48-1984

Address all inquiries to:
NEW FALCON PUBLICATIONS
1739 East Broadway Road #1-277
Tempe, AZ 85282 U.S.A.
(or)
320 East Charleston Blvd. • #204-286
Las Vegas, NV 89104 U.S.A.
website: http://www.newfalcon.com
email: info@newfalcon.com

It is my belief that all presenting problems and symptoms are really metaphors that contain a story about what the problem really is. It is, therefore, the responsibility of the therapist to create metaphors that contain a story that contains the (possible) solutions. The metaphor is the message... Hypnosis is, in and of itself, a metaphor within a metaphor...

— Steven Heller, Ph.D.

Table of Contents

Foreword

Once upon a time, in a far off land, there was a man known as the "Weaver of Fabrics." People would come to the weaver with their yarns of many colors—yarns they had collected for many, many years. And the weaver would help each person learn how to weave the yarns into beautiful tapestries, each with a unique pattern to be used in many different ways.

Steve Heller, together with the help of his dear friend and colleague Terry Steele, has provided readers with a dynamic and brilliant entrance into a magical world within each of us—a world where it is believed our true abilities, inner learnings, and healing resources reside. Through the use of humor, metaphor, and enlightening case examples, Heller takes us far beyond the conscious world of what we "think" and "perceive" reality to be, and stretches our minds into the dimension known as the *unconscious*. His original, and often provocative, theories and approaches help shed new light on the classic question confronting many of us: "Why can't I overcome my problem when I'm so competent in other areas of my life? Why am I continually stuck in this area?"

Heller's views take us into a powerful realm within the unconscious mind that not only perpetuates the problems, but also contains solutions. It is here that Heller offers the field of psychotherapy a major contribution: his conceptualization of the "unconscious/out-of-conscious" sensory system finally provides clinicians with a tangible and precise means of working with the elusive and problematic aspects of unconscious functioning. By creatively evoking, assessing, and utilizing the language of our sensory systems, Heller is able to identify the out-of-conscious sensory system that is generating the system, pain, or unwanted behavior. He then shows us how he playfully and hypnotically helps clients enter into their own out-of-conscious sensory systems to bring back into conscious awareness the innate resources of this pivotal area.

This process facilitates the clients' discoveries of choices in their lives, and activates their abilities to break unwanted patterns of feeling and behavior. What was once creating the problem—out-of-conscious sensory system—now becomes an ally and a resource for generating growth, not only within the previous problem area, but into other areas of life as well.

Those who would see the beautiful fabrics with unique patterns wanted to know who was their teacher. "The Weaver of Fabrics," the people would answer proudly. And so the legend of the Weaver grew and spread throughout the land.

Joyce C. Mills, Ph.D.
Encino, California

Richard J. Crowley, Ph.D.
North Hollywood, California

Introduction

Nothing is.
Nothing becomes.
Nothing is not.
— Aleister Crowley, *The Book of Lies*

Although I have been using a form of "hypnosis" for more than fifteen years now, I found this book by Steven Heller and Terry Lee Steele not only illuminating, but intellectually staggering. It occurs to me that I have never really understood "hypnosis" before.

When I was first taught "hypnosis," it was called "guided meditation," and was supposed to be a sort of synthesis of psychoanalysis and Buddhism, bringing one rapidly to the bedrock of consciousness. Then I was taught it all over again, but it was called "astral projection" and was supposed to be literal journeys of some literal "ego" outside the body. By then I was being asked to lead seminars myself, and began including some of these techniques without making any specific claims about them except that they showed some unusual properties of the human mind. Since I had no degree at the time, if the word "hypnosis" was raised at all, I always said that we were using "guided meditation," which was only somewhat similar to very *mild* "hypnosis." I did not want anybody to think they were going into *deep hypnosis,* since I was not sure I knew how to handle that.

Well, of course, many people very obviously went into "deep hypnosis" whether I intended it or not, and I learned eventually that I could handle that, and I got a degree and was qualified to mess with people's minds. But somehow "hypnosis"—whether "mild" or "deep"—always seemed a bit weird to me and I preferred to work with techniques I thought I understood better.

Now I have read Heller and Steele and realize that I am using "hypnosis" all the time, whether I know it or not. But then, it appears that every salesperson, every lawyer, every politician, every cop, and every husband and wife having a quarrel, are using "hypnosis" as well as they know how and the world is, in many respects, a circus with rival gangs of hypnotists trying to hypnotize one another.

Of course, some of this is not entirely new to me. Several years ago, bothered by a set of "allergy" symptoms that puzzled my physician, I was persuaded to try a Christian Science healer. I was healed in one session. The alleged "allergy" has never come back. This was not only gratifying, but also aroused my curiosity, and I began reading a great deal of Christian Science literature. (I even went to their church services a few times, but my allergy to churches seems incurable, and that phase did not last long.) I then began experimenting on myself, using what I understood of Christian Science to heal other ailments when the symptoms did not appear so serious that it was obvious damnfoolery to avoid medical treatment. I found that I could heal quite a few minor conditions in myself, and once or twice in friends. I did not set up shop as a psychic healer or anything of that sort because I seemed to have only minor talent in that field, but I suspect that everybody has as much of that talent as I do, but most people are just afraid to try using it.

What is comical about this little story of my mediocre career in faith healing is that the principles I learned from Mrs. Eddy's books and her disciples are the same principles you will learn in the following text, but Mrs. Eddy never admitted she was using hypnosis. In fact, one whole chapter of *Science and Health* is devoted to denouncing hypnosis and hypnotists. Hypnosis, she thought, was the work of the devil (who doesn't exist) and Christian Science is the work of God (who does exist) and hence hypnosis does not work, but Christian Science does. The Strange Loop in that logic is typical of Christian Science-and of many other systems that use hypnosis without realizing what they are doing.

I think you will gain even more insight into why Dr. Heller explains the success of hypnosis by saying, "There is no such thing as hypnosis?" if you pick up a copy of Mrs. Eddy's Science and Health somewhere and read ten consecutive pages (any ten pages will do, since her style is hologrammic and the meaning is everywhere). After ten pages in Eddyland come back and read a little of Dr. Heller again. You might begin to understand that there literally is no such thing as hypnosis and we are all in deep hypnosis more of the time than we realize.

Since I am a devout believer in synchronicity, I paused while writing these words and picked up another book I happen to be reading at this time to check the Jungian hypothesis that, if I opened it at random, I would find a text that makes the above point even clearer. The book I used for this experiment is *The Politics of Irish Freedom,* by Gerry Adams, who is President of Sinn Fein, a political party widely rumored to be a "front" for the I.R.A. (although Sinn Fein, of course, denies this). This is the passage I found in the ideological exposition of Mr. Adams, who happens to be a member of the British Parliament whether or not he is also a "front" for the Irish Republican Army:

> There is no such thing as a neutral language, for language is the means by which culture, the totality of our response to the world we live in, is communicated, and for that reason the Irish language had to be destroyed. When a people have spoken a common language for thousands of years that language reflects their history, sentiments, outlook and philosophy.

Mr. Adams goes on to discuss the *bata scoir,* which was a stick used in 19th Century schools in Ireland. Each time a child spoke Irish, he or she was hit with the stick, and the stick was then notched to record the number of such offenses. Some would call this cultural imperialism or brainwashing or something like that, but few would call it "hypnosis." Nonetheless, the number of Irish speakers in Ireland decreased from nearly 100 percent circa 1800 to around five percent circa 1900 and a whole culture or reality-tunnel died in the process.

There was no *bata scoir* employed in the United States when I was in my teens, but some similar and more subtle training device was used on the minds of my generation. When I entered high school, the Germans and Japanese were the bad guys in the world, and the Russians were our gallant allies in the war against fascism. By the time I got out of high school, the Russians were the bad guys and the Germans and the Japanese were our gallant allies in the war against communism. Whether you call this conditioning or hypnosis (but there is no such thing as hypnosis...), it worked with the majority of that generation. One reality-tunnel was extinguished and a new one was imprinted in its place.

(For some techniques to explore your own reality-tunnels, get my books *Prometheus Rising* and *Quantum Psychology;* and for those of you who want to do some self-reprogramming, check out Antero Alli's *Angel Tech: A Modern Shaman's Guide to Reality Selection,* and Christopher Hyatt's brilliant *Undoing Yourself with Energized Meditation.* New Falcon Publications will appreciate it and so will I.)

Between 1970 and 1980 I lived in Northern California. Although there are some "redneck" or "moral majority" enclaves even there, in the cities where I lived virtually everybody was some kind of radical—a political radical, a philosophical radical or a radical therapist. Abortion was a civil right. There was no legal gambling anywhere, although I hear that has been liberalized a bit since I left. Bisexuality was a permissible variation and very commonly seen. Science and Eastern mysticism were about to merge in some New Paradigm which would combine the best of both global and brain hemispheres. Socialism, however, was the opinion only of an eccentric minority, and pacifism, although universally respected in our crowd, never had any influence on the national government.

But there is no such thing as hypnosis.

In the last five years, I have lived in Ireland. Abortion is illegal, and even telling a patient where abortions may be obtained in England can cause a doctor to be prosecuted. Gambling on the other hand has been legal as far back as anybody remembers. Bisexuality, if it exists, has only vaguely been heard of, and homosexuality is known to be very offensive to the Deity who invented AIDS to punish the bloody sodomites. Science and Eastern mysticism are hardly known, and the possibility of their joining in synergy arouses the blank stares that you might expect if you said a bicycle and a cow were about to mate and reproduce. On the other hand, two of the five largest political parties are openly socialist (the Labour Party and the Workers Party) and one of those two (Labour) was part of the most recent coalition government; Ireland is surrounded by socialist states all over Europe, and cannot understand why Americans think socialism is diabolical and impossible. As for pacifism, it is written into the constitution and all five major parties are officially pacifist: no legislation contrary to Irish neutrality is ever even introduced into Dad hEriann (the Parliament).

And yet there is no such thing as hypnosis.

There are, around the world, people living in reality-tunnels which cause them to think that both the Californian and the Irish reality-tunnels are insane or perverse. There are nudists and Buddhists and Russian communists and Albanian communists and Norse socialists and French existentialists and Samoan shamans and New York Jewish intellectuals and all of them know, for sure, that they happen to have the one correct reality-tunnel.

And yet there is no such thing as hypnosis.

Christian Science works by Faith in God. Political and religious differences are caused by indoctrination or some mysterious process called "brainwashing." All that "astral projection" I mentioned earlier just shows that occultists are very neurotic people easily prone to hallucinations.

In *Programming and Metaprogramming in the Human Biocomputer,* Dr. John Lilly points out in three sentences something that is totally obvious once stated, and yet will totally revolutionize your world once you begin to really understand it:

> In the Province of the mind, what is believed true is true or becomes true, within limits to be found experimentally and experientially. These limits are further beliefs to be transcended. In the province of the mind there are no limits.

Timothy Leary used to say it even more simply, back in the 1960s: *You can be anything you want to be, this time around.*

It is hard to believe that a whole culture could be destroyed when the Irish language was destroyed, and yet that happened. It is hard to believe that an allergy can go away when a Christian Science practitioner says it is gone, and yet that happened. It is hard to believe that there is no such thing as hypnosis although we are all hypnotizing ourselves and one another all the time, and yet that is what is happening every day and why "we" are afraid that "we" are about to blow ourselves to hell with nuclear bombs.

A neighbor once came to Nasrudin, the great Sufi sage or swindler (is there a difference?). "Can I borrow some flour?" he asked.

"I'd like to loan it to you," Nasrudin said, "but unfortunately I have it drying on the clothesline right now."

"But," the man protested, "how can you dry flour on a clothesline?"

"It's easy when you don't want to loan any," Nasrudin replied.

If you don't understand that story and wonder how even a Sufi can dry flour on a clothesline, read the following pages carefully. It will all be clear when you finish. Then go read those ten pages from Mrs. Eddy.

If it is still not clear that there are no limits in the province of the mind, get a copy of Phil Laut's book, *Money Is My Friend,* which tells you how to become rich and stop worrying about money. Analyze what the Laut system has in common with this book and Christian Science. If you are still puzzled, think about all this very deeply and slowly one more time and then turn on the television at the time when all the channels have their commercial breaks. You will soon see how easy it is to dry flour on a clothesline. You might even see who creates the clothesline that makes such marvels possible.

Robert Anton Wilson
Dublin, Ireland
23 January 1987

Fore-Warned/Acknowledgements

When an individual wanders into a new area and is bitten by a dog, that is an unfortunate accident. However, when a sign has been posted that says, "Beware of Dog" and the individual wanders in anyway and is bitten...well we could label that something else. As you wander into the new areas of this book be advised that it is my intention to "bite" you. You have now been duly warned.

It has been my experience that most individuals who read books on hypnosis are looking for a cookbook with exact recipes. For those of you who believe that you need a cookbook, I recommend any book in the "Betty Crocker" series. You will not find the exact recipes here. Even with a cookbook, a master chef knows that making changes in the recipes is the difference between an average cook and a great one. A great cook is one that is creative and who adjusts the recipes according to circumstances.

I hope that as you read this work you will decide to be a creative cook... Use what you may learn as a guide, but not as an exact road map. Feel free to add, subtract, divide and change the ingredients to suit the "meal" you wish to serve and to fit the company that will be sitting at your "table."

In the course of conducting my training seminars, Clinical Hypnosis: Innovative Techniques®, I have often been asked what it takes to be an effective hypnotist. My response has been, and is, "You must learn the necessary tools and techniques that help direct individuals to their own inner resources and creativity. Once you have done that, you must then get the hell out of their way." I give that response because I believe that each one of us has within, all the tools and solutions necessary for a more effective life. We sometimes just need some help in knowing where to look. We often spend too much time and energy trying to figure out where other people are. A compass has 360 degrees, and if we do not know where we are, we have 359 chances out of 360 to go where we don't want to be in the first place.

To the above, someone will respond, "If that's what being a good hypnotist is, what good is hypnosis itself?" My reply: "Hypnosis helps get the individual out of their own way!" In most cases of so-called dysfunction, the individual has been following their own footsteps in a circle. It is as if they were in a hurry to catch their own ass. When they fail to catch that part of their anatomy, they act as if they are failures. On the other hand, when they succeed, they end up suffering from chronic "Head Up the Assitis."

It is the intention of Terry and myself to help you have the tools necessary to help people remove their heads from that rather dark place. In building a new structure, or in remodeling an old one, you do not want to attempt putting up the roof before you have built the walls. Of course, you don't want to put up the walls until you have completed the foundation; never build the foundation on quicksand. It is our hope that this book will be general blueprint for constructing flexible structure upon a solid foundation.

I know that I am not unique in finding it difficult as to whom and in what order I want to thank for their contributions. To those I failed to mention, and to those I have not given the proper credit, I apologize. As to those individuals I have mentioned, what I can write cannot come close to what I feel as to your contributions and efforts.

The first and most important person I wish to thank is my co-author Terry Lee Steele. If not for Terry, I doubt that I would have continued this work to its conclusion. In addition to her direct contributions, there was her well-placed foot in the proper part of my body, "gently" reminding me to work, and then work some more. In addition, the "Bullshit" tasks that she, with unfailing good nature, tackled, made this book possible. She is not only a delightful person, but also a talented, dedicated individual who is rapidly becoming a "therapist's therapist."

I would like to thank my friend and colleague, James Walker, Ph.D., not merely for wading through my misspellings and improper sentence structure, but also for raising several good questions that needed answers. His questions led to the rewrite of several chapters. For this extra work he helped to produce, I can only say (censored). I also wish to extend a special thanks to H. Brian Herdeg, M.D. To me, Brian is a unique physician, not only in the level of care (medical and personal) that he delivers to his patients, but also for his willingness to open up to new methods and approaches. While many physicians had, in the past, "snuck" patients to me, Brian was the first to openly accept whatever it is that I do. In addition, he has "lobbied" to get other physicians to accept my methodologies, and has helped to present me to professional groups. He has also been instrumental in getting me into a hospital setting without subterfuge. (In the past, I was brought in as some relative of the patient.) He has done all this without personal gain of any sort. For his confidence, trust and, most important, his friendship, thanks.

I would like to extend a special thank you to a special lady, Susan Song. She has not only put up with the trials and tribulations of this book, but, more importantly, with *me*. Susan has read and re-read and then re-re-read rough (very rough) drafts of this book. She made several suggestions that have helped me clarify where I was going. She has also contributed to the organization of my seminars, and the "nitty-gritty" stuff in general. Without her contributions, I would have been buried in an avalanche of fertilizer.

We would like to extend a special acknowledgment to John Grinder and Richard Bandler, known to many as Bandler and Grinder or simply B and G. Their pioneering work, in what has come to be known as "SYSTEMS and ANCHORING" not only made our work easier, but, even more importantly, paved the road for many to travel.

While we are not "NLPers," there are areas in this work that draw on or overlap the NLP approach. The differences between our methodology and NLP, while substantial, merely add spice to the recipe. B and G's main contribution to the senior author was to "give you a map that will make it easier to do what you are already doing in your clinical setting" (Richard Grinder, personal communication 1975).

In addition to the people I have already mentioned, there are many more I wish to thank. To all those individuals who have allowed me to "mess" around with their heads, thank you for your trust. I know I have learned as much from you as I hope you have learned from me. To all those professionals who have trusted me enough to train with me and to refer their patients, thank you. To the several hundreds of you who have attended my seminars, thank you for your support and encouragement. A special thanks to those "terminal" patients who have allowed me to work with them, for reminding me who I am, and what is really important.

Last, but not least, there are some others I wish to acknowledge. My sister, Marsha Pearlman, for her efforts in the final typing and preparation of this manuscript; Dr. Jack Klausen and Glori Klausen, first for their personal friendship and secondly for their efforts to introduce my methods and me to hospitals, professionals and ancillary staff; Dr. Robert Reed for our friendship and for his trust, and for his efforts at introducing my programs to his unique corner of the world; a new friend and colleague, Dr. Ed Aronson for becoming my "press agent" in his efforts to make my programs available to more people.

Steven Heller
February 1987

When I first heard Steve talk about his work, I knew he had some of the missing pieces to the hypnosis puzzle that I was searching for and working to develop. Throughout our years of association, I have been both student and colleague. A persistent student, persuading Steve to assume the role of teacher, to define, guide, and share his insights. An excited colleague, wanting to get those puzzle pieces collected and pieced together so a more complete picture of hypnotic communication would be available and evident to others.

Writing this book with Steve has been an interesting experience. It has also been educational, frustrating, and an elaborate test of patience. I was determined to create a book that gave details, explanations, and provided basic principles and guidelines for applications in the therapy situation. Steve was equally determined not to produce a cookbook type of book that leads the reader to believe that a magic, all-purpose, recipe exists. It does not. I believe we have succeeded.

My hope is that as you read it you are enlightened, encouraged, and entertained. And, having read it, that you begin to creatively integrate knowledge, technique, and intuition.

My gratitude goes to Shirley Coleman for hours of typing and clever memos, and to all the family, friends, colleagues, and clients who provided impetus and moral support. A special thank you to Mike Dicken who is a constant source of strength, encouragement, and joy.

Terry Lee Steele

I

Into Hypnosis Lightly

HYPNOSIS — THE FIRST STEP

There's No Such Thing As Hypnosis? may appear to be a strange subtitle for a book written by a man who has been in the field of clinical hypnosis for many years. The title is sure to displease those who firmly believe that hypnosis exists, and the book itself will displease those who firmly believe that hypnosis does *not* exist. I firmly believe that hypnosis is just a state...South of Oregon and North of Washington, and it doesn't really exist except in people's minds. Paul Watzlawick, in his excellent book, *The Language of Change* states, "There's no such thing as piano playing; I have tried it several times and nothing came of it." One major problem in discussing or writing about the process of hypnosis is that, through the years, so many definitions of what hypnosis is or is not have been hooked into the word itself, that people have preconceived notions and ideas. It might be said that they have been hypnotized into believing whatever it is they believe about hypnosis.

It is not the purpose of this book to give an academic definition of hypnosis. There are many fine texts and case books that do an excellent job of giving several different and conflicting definitions of hypnosis. These definitions, people are free to reject or not accept as they see fit. If, however, hypnosis means a special state in which a person is put into some deep mystical state and then loses volition over their being because another person, called a hypnotist, creates such powerful, overwhelming suggestions that the victim or subject is helpless to resist, then there is no such thing as hypnosis. If that "power" existed, I would not be writing this book nor working at my profession. I would simply walk into any large corporation and cause the chief executive officer to give me the business. If, however, we consider hypnosis as a generic term that encompasses all forms of altered consciousness, and do not consider hypnosis as a mystical state, we may then get a more clear picture that feels more comfortable.

To further illustrate the use of the word "hypnosis" as a generic term that encompasses many states, let us consider a state called sleep. We recognize there is light sleep, deep sleep, REM sleep, restless sleep, etc. However, all of these are contained under the category called "sleep." Experts still argue over just what produces sleep and why people sleep in so many ways, but no one denies the existence of the sleep state. If you will picture a horizontal line and think of one end as conscious awareness and the other as sleep, you then can envision and grasp the many gradients between these two opposite points. You might accept hypnosis as an area between these two poles at which an individual's awareness of his surroundings are diminished, while awareness of internal processes, feelings, thoughts and pictures are increased.

Another simile for hypnosis can be found in electricity. We all know that electricity exists, and yet the experts still argue over what electricity really is. The only generally accepted notion is that electricity is a form of energy. You may consider hypnotic techniques as a group of methods for the production of a different form of energy in the brain, and the hypnotic state a conduit for directing that energy toward the accomplishment of goals.

HYPNOSIS AS COMMUNICATION

Included in our definition of hypnosis is any form of communication in which a person or persons, whether a hypnotist, wife, husband, teacher, or? uses words, tonality, expressions or movement that elicit and/or evoke within another person an internal experience, and that experience becomes a reality of its own. For example, if I write or speak the word "rose," you might think of a particular flower, perhaps red in color. I could mean a person named Rose, and someone else might remember someone getting up. If I change the meaning to a beautiful red rose, one person might remember a special occasion, the feelings, sounds, pictures, smells and, in effect, relive the entire experience. Yet another person might make a terrible face because they are allergic to roses.

I can remember an incident during which I was having a conversation with a lovely woman, and another woman came to join us. I suddenly found myself feeling about four years old "seeing" an aunt who, to me, was gargantuan. I felt the fear of being overpowered by her size and "saw" her in a polka dot dress. After a moment, I shook my head and returned to the present to realize that the second woman's perfume reminded me of my aunt's perfume. The smell alone regressed me to that childhood experience. There's no such thing as hypnosis, and you need a deep trance and powerful suggestion to produce regression. Really??? One technique of so-called traditional hypnosis is called "negative hallucination." This is produced by putting someone in a "hypnotic state" and suggesting, for example, that they will not see or hear some person or object. A so-called "good subject" would come out of trance and not see or hear as suggested. How many times have you called your children for dinner and they have responded by not responding?

An individual comes to your office stating, "I can't make a decision; it's just impossible." That, too, is a negative hallucination. That individual *decided* to seek you out, *decided* what route to take, and *decided* to enter into a transaction with you. Or, take the individual who states, "Everybody hates me, they always have." Obviously, if s/he has lived to tell their tale, someone, in all probability, cared for and helped him/her but, s/he has excluded that portion of history from his/her reality. Just because someone makes a face at you, it doesn't mean they're not constipated. Again, there's no such thing as hypnosis; or perhaps it is *all* hypnosis.

A FLAT WORLD

Once upon a time people believed that the world was flat. They were told this by people in authority. As a result, they built their whole world predicated on staying within the confines of a flat world. If we restrict ourselves to the old definitions of hypnosis, then we are experiencing a flat world. Our world becomes round when we step back, see, and hear that so-called hypnotic phenomenon occur all around us without the need of a trance. Someone says to you, "I can't be successful. I always fail." Yet, they know how to walk, they know how to talk, they know how to do those things and more—successfully. We are talking about a belief system, a suggestion or suggestions that have been accepted and acted upon even at the expense of distorting reality.

To recap, if you consider hypnosis as a specific state that always includes a deep trance, then there's no such thing as hypnosis. If, however, you use hypnosis as a generic term to encompass anything that alters perception, or changes consciousness, then you can realize that hypnosis is just a word. Within that word are things like meditation, fantasy, guided imagery, deep muscle relaxation—anything that encourages or precipitates a person's turning inward and having an inner experience that becomes more profound or more important than the outer consensual reality. Since we all live in the same world, and we have, more or less, the same opportunities, it is sad that people use this thing that doesn't exist to convince themselves that their choices do not exist. Hopefully, this book will help you to become aware of how to use these same methods differently; to take the same techniques a person uses to build limits and use those techniques to build new choices and new horizons.

II

Meta 4 — Change — Life

ILLUSIONS

Las Vegas, Nevada. The lights are bright, a feeling of excitement hangs in the air. A young couple, on their first trip, looking forward to learning and playing blackjack, walk into a beautiful casino. They see a player sitting at a blackjack table with thousands of dollars in one hundred dollar chips. They watch and listen with fascination. The player is betting three or four hundred dollars a hand, winning and losing. They study the player's method, see his playing style, until they grasp it all, "knowing" with that much money in front of him he has to be an expert. They take their limited funds, sit down, play and lose everything. They then decide there must be something wrong with them if copying an expert leads to such failure. If only they would talk to the casino manager, they might learn that the "expert" is really the pizza king of Chicago. He knows everything about pizza and nothing about blackjack. He has enough money to buy large sums of chips and appearances are deceiving. Even a monkey will get dealt a winning hand from time to time. The couple's mistake was to assume based on appearances.

Once upon a time, there was a little boy and girl who heard some adults use big words, and saw them do amazing things: drive a car, vote, fight, and much more. The little boy and girl assumed that since they "knew" such things, they must be experts at life and parenting. The little boy and girl set out to copy the adults only to suffer pain and frustration. Those adults were experts at pizza, but the children were too small to look beyond appearances.

25

ROSEBUSHES

Once upon a time there were two little rose bushes named Judy and Jim. These rose bushes were comfortable in a nursery when two people came in and took Judy, claiming they were expert gardeners and knew a great deal about rose bushes—and they did. They planted Judy in rich soil with the best combination of sunshine, water and nourishment. They kept the weeds and bugs away and handled Judy with kindness. Judy flourished and grew big and beautiful roses, and if rose bushes could feel, Judy was happy. Two other people went to the nursery and took Jim, stating they were expert gardeners and knew everything about roses. But, they were really pizza kings from Chicago. They planted Jim in sandy, salty soil, with too much heat in the day and too much cold in the night. They watered Jim too much and then too little, and they did nothing about the weeds and bugs. In spite of these things, Jim survived but was wilted, stunted and sorry looking. Jim looked across the field at Judy and saw her beauty and decided (if a rose bush can decide) that the problem was he was just basically defective and no damn good.

Now, dear reader, if you could talk to a rose bush, I'm confident you would say, "Jim, it's not you! The experts were not experts, and it's your environment that's the problem." But, to what purpose? A little rose bush can't walk, drive a car or work. However, time goes by and Jim, by hook end by crook, learns to walk, talk, drive a car and work. He pulls himself out of the crummy environment and moves to where Judy is: the rich fertile environment and guess what? Wrong! Jim continues to wilt, and grow little, ugly roses. Jim is so convinced that he's defective that he decided, "What's the use? It wouldn't do any good to even try." In addition, he carries his past environment with him and "knows" that the rich environment doesn't exist. Well, what can you expect from a rose bush?

MONKEY BUSINESS

There once was a rhesus monkey who was put into a special cage. This cage had red, yellow and green squares. After several days, an "experimenter" set it up so that the red squares gave off intermittent shocks causing the monkey much pain. The monkey became anxious but soon learned to avoid the red square. Next, the experimenter caused the red and yellow squares to give off intermittent shocks, and the monkey acted as if he was a manic depressive, alternating from hyper-anxiety to depression and withdrawal. The monkey soon learned to avoid the red and yellow squares and then *all* the squares were electrified. The little monkey began to bite itself, beat its head against the bars and defecated on himself. You might say the little monkey had been driven crazy. This experiment took one month. He was then transferred to a second cage with a white floor. Soft music was played, he was touched and held and fed. Within a short time, he calmed down and within two weeks he was playful and exploring his cage. He could not be seen as different from a monkey from a rhesus population that had not been subjected to the experiment. Well, what do you expect from a dumb monkey? He's not as smart as a man. He didn't know how to hold onto the past forever, nor continue to anticipate disaster. He only knew how to adapt to changing circumstances. When he was put back into the first cage, he was anxious for two days, but, after assuring himself there were no shocks, he began to be as playful in that cage, too.

Well, as I've pointed out, monkeys aren't as smart as men. Maybe just smarter than rose bushes.

If, as you read the above meta-eights—a metaphor within a metaphor within a metaphor—you found yourself thinking, remembering, connecting, seeking, and understanding, it was only intended. To understand a metaphor, you must, in most cases, go into your own history, remember those situations that look similar and remember those words...

But there's "know" such thing as hypnosis.

III

Everyday Hypnosis/Learning

WAKING HYPNOSIS

One evening, a group of friends and I were having dinner at a local restaurant. Our waiter was very distracted and he appeared to be agitated and depressed. He was abrupt, slow and unfriendly. As a result, our service left a great deal to be desired. Since I wanted to have an enjoyable evening, I decided to "talk funny" to him in order to help him feel better. As he walked by our table holding a coffee pot, I touched his arm and said, "I'm sorry that you forgot that special night...with that special person...those exciting things that happened...those very warm feelings that would embarrass you to talk about...since we are all strangers." For a moment his face went blank; he looked up to his left; his face then lit up and he said, "How do you know about that?" He then smiled and began to laugh, and his whole attitude changed as if by magic. He said, "Wow. That was some night. I don't know how you know about it."

The next time he came to our table, I said to him, "Wasn't it simply amazing that when you remember those happy, warm feelings, your attitude continues to change, and you continue to feel even better?" We received delightful service throughout the rest of the evening. What was even nicer, was that as we left he told us that we were one of the nicest parties he had ever waited on. He also asked us to be sure to ask for him whenever we returned. Now, I have absolutely no idea as to what he hallucinated, but my communication resulted in his going back into his own history. He then found an experience that filled in the blanks, and that memory helped him to change his whole attitude in a matter of seconds. Of course, there's no such thing as hypnosis, and if there is, he should have gone deeper and deeper into a trance.

HYPNOTIC TRANSACTIONS

One classical definition of hypnotic suggestion is: using words that cause the subject to go back in time and recover a memory that causes an emotional affect. If we accept that as a definition of hypnotic suggestion, then my communication, and the waiter's response, would fit very well. My communication left him with basically two choices: to ask me what the hell I was talking about, or to respond just as he did. I believe that these types of hypnotic transactions occur much more often than most people would believe. They (hypnotic communication and responses) are even more common in an emotionally charged environment. The therapy arena is one such environment.

A patient enters a therapist's office, sits down and says, "I am really down today. I went out on a date last night, and my date really hurt me." The therapist responds, "I understand. That really feels bad." What specifically does the therapist understand? Is the therapist remembering a time s/he was "hurt" because his/her date said, "Don't bother to call me, I'll call you?" or, "I don't want to hurt you, but I am in love with your best friend"? Perhaps the patient means that his/her date hit him/her on the head with a hammer. In response to the statement "...my date really hurt me," the therapist hallucinated...filled in with pictures, feelings and responses from his/her own history. Who is hypnotizing whom? The above transaction would come pretty close to fitting the definition of a hypnotic transaction. In the therapy milieu, it is my belief that you either use the tool called hypnosis, or you will end up being hypnotized by the people who are paying you to help them.

ENTRANCING TONES

If we understand the word "hypnosis" to mean only a trance state, then our ability to recognize hypnotic transactions will be severely limited. If, however, we use the word hypnosis to imply any transaction and communication that causes an individual to go into their own experiences and call upon their own imagination in order to respond, we will have a map that will allow us to become aware of the hypnotic transactions occurring around us. In addition, if we begin to accept that these transactions can be "triggered" by not only words, but also visual cues, tones, people and things, then our map will be even more helpful.

A colleague and myself were training a psychiatric resident in the use of hypnosis. He brought us a video tape of his work with a "schizophrenic." He told us that he was not only having trouble working with that patient, but that by the end of the session, he was a nervous wreck. As we watched his tape, I began to laugh, which upset him even more. I stopped the tape and pointed out that his patient was being very successful in hypnotizing him. I started the tape from the beginning and helped him to see what I meant. The patient was sitting in a way I can best describe as a pretzel. He was also talking "word salad" with many pauses between words. Within a few minutes, the resident was "copying" the patient: sitting in the same way; jumping from one idea to another; pausing between words, and with growing evidence of anxiety. Another way of describing their transaction would be as follows: the patient was using words, tones and so-called body language, and the resident was responding like a perfect hypnotic subject. By becoming aware of what was happening, the resident was able to interrupt what the patient was doing and to begin to get the patient to follow him.

A woman entered my office very depressed and upset. She told me that her husband had called her a fat pig. I thought it was unkind for him to have said that, but I also thought that there were more graceful ways for her to handle it, rather than becoming so depressed. As I began to probe just how and when he had said it, it turned out that he had not used those words at all. She had heard "that" tone of voice and "knew" just what he meant.

> People do not passively "register" the sentences uttered by a speaker. Instead they hear what they *expect* to hear. They actively reconstruct both the *sounds* and syntax of the utterance in accordance with their expectations.   — Aitchison, 1976

TO REGRESS

I asked her to close her eyes and "remember that tone...until you are feeling those feelings that let you know that he is calling you a 'fat pig.' When you have those feelings, signal me by raising the first finger of your left hand." After a minute or two, she signaled and I said, "Now see his face...looking just as it did then...while you hear that tone. Now, let his face fade away and be replaced by that other person who used that tone at some other time in your life, and who used words like 'fat pig.'" She was able to discover that her husband's tone (when he was angry) reminded her exactly of her father's tone of voice when he was angry. She also recalled that he (her father) actually called her mother a fat pig, and told her she was getting to be just like her mother. So, when she heard her husband's tone of voice, she disconnected from consensual reality, went into her inner reality, filled in words from out of the past, responded to those words as if they had been said, and became depressed. All that based on what had happened many years before. Aitchison (cited) in discussing Psycholinguistics, stated:

> ...it is not only a person's expectation of sound patterns that influences what she hears, but perhaps to an even greater extent, her expectation of syntactic and semantic patterns.... When someone hears a sentence, she latches on to outline clues, and "jumps to conclusions" about what she is hearing.

Now, let us examine one hypnotic phenomenon called regression. A hypnotist will use words (suggestions) designed to cause the subject to "go back" in time in order to re-experience some past event or to examine some past event. Where this "regression" is successful, the subject will react, at least emotionally, as if the past event is happening in the present. If we examine the transaction between the woman and her husband, and what occurred as a result of his "tone of voice," it would match the definition of a hypnotic regression. Of course, the woman was not in a trance. Or was she? As she explained what had happened to "make her depressed," she began to stare straight ahead. As she really got into her story, I observed that her eyes had dilated, her breathing and color had changed, and her eyes had become glazed. When I slowly moved my hand across her line of vision, she didn't even see it. Any person who had been trained in the basics of hypnotic phenomena would have been able to see that she was in a trance. If her mere retelling of what had happened produced a hypnotic state, we can wonder what the incident itself might have produced.

In the "real" world of everyday life, hypnotic communications and transactions take place all around you. As you open yourself up to the many possibilities, I am sure you will begin to see more of them. What of the parent who gives a small child a "dirty" look and says, "You'd better clean up your room or else," and then walks away leaving the child to wonder, "Or else what? The Jolly Green Giant will throw me away?" The child then becomes anxious, agitated and then waits for disaster. What of the child who is told, "What is the matter with you? Can't you do anything right?" and the child begins to think, "I can't do anything right," turning the question into a directive. S/he may even come to

believe that mommy and daddy will be *pleased* if s/he doesn't do anything right. If the child begins to carry out the suggestions often enough,
well, I don't need to tell you what *those* results could be.

HYPNOSIS AND LIFE SCRIPTS

"TA" (Transactional Analysis) therapists follow a concept they call
"Life Scripts." They believe that individuals are given a "script" to
follow, that, if painful and not changed, will cause that individual to act
in ways that are self-defeating. "You can't drink kid, you can't drink
until you are a man." That kind of message can translate unconsciously
into: "To be a man, I have to drink." Here is the implantation of a suggestion that may take such firm hold that the individual ends up an alcoholic. In fact, the "TA" people contend that this is not uncommon.
Another way of looking at this example would be: The words used
caused the individual to fill in his own meaning. This meaning became a
post-hypnotic suggestion, which he later carries out successfully...by
becoming a drunk.

One case reported by a therapist was of a homosexual who, as a
young boy, had been told, "Don't you ever do that [the 'that' being getting caught playing doctor] with girls." He was then beaten with a strap.
The boy translated this transaction into, "It is bad to do this with girls,
but it is OK to do it with boys." Years later he is labeled "homosexual"
as a result of being such a good hypnotic subject.

In the above examples of the alcoholic and the homosexual, we can
find something important to consider. As a result of what I call hypnotic
transactions, those individuals learned to believe certain ideas. From their
ideas, they learned to behave in ways that some would label painful.
Before we go forward, I would like to take you back...to our friend, the
waiter. Several months after the incident I described, I returned to that
restaurant with several friends. As fate would have it, we were given a
table in his section. When he came to get our order, he stopped, stared at
me, and said, "Don't I know you from somewhere?" I replied, "I came
here often in the past." He accepted this explanation and went about his
business. I explained to my friends what I had done with him in the past.
We all agreed he was a friendly and cheerful person. Toward the end of
our meal, he came by and asked us if we wanted anything else. Several
of us ordered coffee. He returned holding the coffee pot, stopped, stared,
smiled, and said, "Now I know who you are. I still don't know how you
knew about all of that." With that he sat down in an empty chair and

began to tell us about how I had reminded him of a certain girl, and now they were engaged. After he finished, I attempted to explain to him what I had done, but he wouldn't believe it. He continued to insist that I had inside information.

Remember now...that when I had "talked funny" to him, he was holding a coffee pot in his hand. Part of what I had said involved the feeling of warmth. In a way I could have never predicted, his mind had made an instant connection to the coffee pot, the incident, the feelings, and me. In short, a one trial learning experience. Seeing me only triggered a small part of the experience. The coffee pot triggered the whole thing. We could call the whole transaction a learning experience. It may have been a weird one, but a learning experience nonetheless. As a point of fact, there are many hypnosis researchers who contend that all learning takes place in a state that is very much like a hypnotic one. Some would even say that learning and hypnosis are merely two different words that describe the same thing.

2 + 2 = HYPNOSIS

Now, if someone were to ask you to add 2 + 2, I am confident that you would respond with the correct answer. If you were asked how you knew the answer, you might reply that you learned it as a child. In other words, the question itself caused you to go back into your personal history and find the "proper" associational connection. You would have done that instantly, without conscious awareness of the process. Another way of stating the 2 + 2 example might be as follows: When you were a child, an individual who was an authority figure—called a teacher— stood in front of your class. S/he wrote on a blackboard 2 + 2 = 4, and verbally repeated that information many times. In addition, s/he asked the class to remember the answer so that when you were asked to add 2 + 2, you would automatically respond, 4. We might agree that the above transaction could be given the labels: teaching and learning. If we examine the transaction more carefully, and from a different perspective, we might also agree that it bears a striking resemblance to the classical definition of "hypnotic suggestion" and "post-hypnotic response." Now...think about the waiter and his pot of coffee and his response. It is as if the pot of coffee had become the trigger (just like the question about 2 + 2) which caused him to go back into his personal history and find the "answer." In this case, the answer was to respond to me with full memory, etc.

Now, speaking of stage hypnosis, a volunteer is brought up on the stage and put into "that" state, and told repeatedly that when s/he hears the snapping of the hypnotist's fingers, s/he will respond by singing *Dixie*. The hypnotist then snaps his/her fingers and the subject responds with the "right answer" by singing *Dixie*. Ask yourself...NOW...other than the shorter time factor involved, what is the difference between "learning" 2 + 2 = 4 and the transaction between the stage hypnotist and the subject?

The stage hypnotist now chooses another volunteer and suggests that when a red light is turned on, the subject will raise her left hand. Several minutes later, the hypnotist turns on the red light, and the subject raises her left hand. So what?! We could call that an example of a post-hypnotic suggestion.

You are driving down a busy street, listening to the radio, and deep into your own thoughts. Suddenly, a traffic light turns red and—guess what? You stop (hopefully) without thought and almost automatically. You might call your action a "conditioned response," and you might contend that it is different from the stage hypnotist red light example. Yet, if the red light/hand raising suggestion and response were repeated several times, you might imagine what the subject would do whenever she saw a red light.

In addition to the definitions of hypnotic transactions and communication you have read thus far, I would like to add: hypnosis is a form of education. Ideas, beliefs, possibilities, fantasies, and much more, may be "suggested" and, if accepted, and acted upon several times, they may become a conditioned part of your behavior. In addition, under certain circumstances, a conditioned response can be established in one trial without repetition, and without "practice." Again, think about the waiter. We never "practiced" his response, or my "suggestion," and yet months later, he responded. It is my belief that all behaviors, useful or not, are learned via some kind of hypnotic transaction.

CASE I: SELF-DESTRUCTIVE

A bright and talented young man was referred to me with the presenting problem of "always blowing his opportunities." Prior to seeing me, he had been in formal therapy for two years searching for the answer to his problem. His problem had been labeled as characterlogical disorder. He had also been told that he had tendencies toward sociopathy and self-destruction. (Actually, he talked more like a psychiatrist than a "patient.") He had completed one full year of college with a 4.0 average. He had attempted to complete his second year three times, but, due to his dismal performance, he had been forces to drop out each time. Due to his obvious talents and intelligence, he had been hired by several companies in various management training capacities. This, in spite of his not having completed college. However, each time he was given a promotion, or his position was to be made permanent, he would go on a drunk, miss work and end up getting fired. In one instance, he had gone so far as to attack and injure his immediate superior.

The young man had been raises within a strict, European-style environment in which the father was the unquestioned head of the family. He was very afraid of his parents, and, as a child, like most children, he believed that they knew everything. As a student in the American system, he was encouraged to ask questions. Whenever he questioned his father on any subject, he would be met with a verbal assault, and, in many cases, he would be punished. While in a formal state of hypnosis (whatever that is), he recovered a very clear visual image: he saw his mother standing over him, pointing a finger at him, and screaming. He was then able to "hear" her words: "Don't you ever try to be better than your father." He was able to recall his feelings of terror and impending doom. The fact that his father was a retired mailman who had never attended college is probably not...VERY IMPORTANT. Since there's no such thing as hypnosis, it is just a coincidence that every time he was about to go beyond his father, something happened which stopped him from being better than his father. He was a very good boy. He was merely doing what his mother had told him.

Let us assume that a part of our young man recognizes his talents and potential and wants to use them, while another part of him says, "What are you trying to do guy? Be better than your father and lose your mother's love?" (or whatever). This conflict could produce a classical approach/avoidance conflict. The closer he gets to becoming successful, the closer he gets to "being better" than his father, the more he runs into past suggestions and their attendant fears. The further he runs from using his talents and abilities, the more his successful part starts pushing him. The results are stress, pain, fear and repeated failure no matter which way he turns. Of course, since his mother did not use a crystal ball to put him into a trance, no hypnosis was involved ... REALLY?

ANXIETY AND HYPNOSIS

Now, let us go back to our metaphoric stage hypnotist. We could imagine him giving the following suggestion: "When I pull on my tie just once, you will raise your left hand. When I pull on my tie twice, you will lower your left hand." We could define this transaction as the giving of a post-hypnotic suggestion to be triggered by a specific visual cue (the pulling of the tie).

A man walks into a party and sees a woman looking at him in a "funny" way. His heart begins to pound; his stomach knots; his palms begin to sweat; he panics, and hurriedly walks out of the party saying to himself, "I can't handle 'this'"—whatever "this" is to him. If we step back and examine that transaction, we could conclude that something he "saw" in her face triggered his responses. In effect, the way she was looking at him acted "as if" a visual cue that triggered his response. (Just like the stage hypnotist pulling on his tie.) His response may, in fact, have little or nothing to do with the reality of the situation. The woman may even have difficulty with her eyes and was "looking at him in that way" because she was having trouble seeing him. Dr. Max Hamilton (1955) addresses this subject in relationship to anxiety states when he stated:

> Thus the patient suffering from an anxiety state may not be able to describe the situation that provokes the anxiety; i.e., it may appear to him that his anxiety is without cause.
> This awareness of the relation of past experience to present experience is fundamental, for it implies that every conscious experience is modified by past experience; i.e., the actual event of experiencing is partly determined by past experience. This is equivalent to saying that no emotion is twice experienced in exactly the same way. Thus, all behavior, including its emotional aspect, is learned behavior.

It is my firm belief that our problems and limitations (as well as our successful attitudes and behaviors) are the result of some form of hypnotic transaction/communication. In the Clinical Hypnosis: Innovative Techniques® training seminars, I have demonstrated that so-called "hypnotic phenomena" can be produced not only via words, but through facial expressions, body postures, certain tonalities, and by merely staring. These experiences have led me to conclude that hypnosis is a method of communication which need not be limited to words alone, but rather may take a multitude of forms.

I CAN'T — I WON'T

If a man were to appear at your office suffering the following complaints: terminal cancer, his wife has run off with the milkman, his son is being tried for murder, and the bank has just foreclosed on his home, we might agree that his problems are reality problems. It would be fair to say that logical, reality problem-solving would be in order. Where can he go for treatment of his cancer? How can he go about getting the necessary legal advice? What steps does he need to consider and in what order? However, the average client or patient who appears at a clinician's office is not often suffering from such "reality" problems, nor are they in such dire straits. In all probability, their reality situation is not substantially different from that of a general cross section of people. Yet, these individuals maybe anxious, depressed, or even "acting" psychotic. If we consider the possibility that their presenting problems are the result of some form of hypnotic transaction, then their problems are not based on logic or reality (much like the man at the party who ran because "she" looked at him in a "funny" way). To attempt to apply logical solutions to illogical (and probably hypnotic) problems is, in my opinion, *ILLOGICAL* therapy.

A man says to his therapist, "I can't go out and meet women!" Obviously, he has seen other men meet women. If the therapist says, "Come on, John, other men meet women. You have met women in your life. You really ought to try it." that therapist has goofed. John probably knows all of "that" and has no doubt heard that "logical advice" before. If logic were the answer, he would have solved his problem, and would be using his money for more enjoyable endeavors than therapy. How logical is it for an individual to raise their hand when a hypnotist pulls on his tie? Why not be *illogical*? Tell the man to go out and get rejected by at least ten women, but to take careful notes as to his responses. Paul Watzlawick (1978), in confronting the issue of logical versus more creative approaches, stated:

> ...Then it also reveals the inappropriatenesss of a procedure which essentially consists in translating this analogic language into the digital language of explanation, argument, analysis, confrontation, interpretation, and so forth, and which, through translation, repeats the mistake which made the sufferer seek help in the first place instead of learning the patient's right-hemispheric (hypnotic) language and utilizing it as the royal road to therapeutic change.

(For those of you who would like a more complete description of illogical methods that work, may I recommend Dr. Watzlawick's fine book, *The Language of Change.*)

I believe that hypnosis is the "language of the right hemisphere" and, therefore, a royal road to therapeutic change.

SVENGALI AND TRILBY

If we begin to realize that words, and other forms of communication, may cause an individual to turn inward and create a hallucinated world to which the individual responds, we have broadened our concept of hypnosis itself. If that hallucinated world is one in which choices are reduced or excluded, and the individual is conditioned to respond in set ways, we would also have a better understanding of hypnotic suggestion and phenomena. Of course, there will be those that say, "That can't be hypnosis. The person was not in a trance. No one was wearing a cape, and no one used a crystal ball."

A question for you, the reader, is: Just when did Svengali and Trilby live? For those of you who are not sure, we can limit the time frame to between this day and sometime in the past. Give up?

In reality, Svengali and Trilby never lived. They were the product of a novelist's imagination. Yet, there are many people who have been hypnotized into believing that they were real. But, of course, lest we forget, there's no such thing as hypnosis...or perhaps it is all hypnosis.

I would like to bring back our metaphoric friend, the stage hypnotist. When we left him, he was giving his subject the following suggestion: "When I pull on my tie once, you will raise your left hand. When I pull on it twice, you will lower your hand." Now, where that "suggestion" is accepted by the subject, we can expect that s/he will respond as requested. If the signal is given often enough, the poor subject will develop a conditioned response. Those who have been trained in traditional hypnotic phenomena will recognize the following: each time the signal is given, the subject will respond in a set, stereotyped sequence of steps. Each individual's responses may be different from that of another, but each will respond in a set, almost compulsive fashion. Now, what I have trouble understanding is this: how does the hypnotic subject's stereotypical responses differ from that of so-called *neurotic* responses? The "neurotic," upon certain conditions, (signals/cues) tends to respond in a set, stereotyped, compulsive way. What, pray tell, is the difference?

IV

Forget It

AMNESIA REMEMBERED

Before it's forgotten completely, I would like to bring up the subject of amnesia and its relationship to the subject of this book. Freud defined amnesia as the repression of traumatic material that the ego (I might call it the conscious mind) is not capable of handling. If we accept that definition as accurate, it would be safe to assume that the traumatic information is still there, but the individual has no conscious awareness of the trauma. If that trauma is still there, then in all probability the affect and the consequences are still active. However, due to the amnesia, the individual will experience unpleasant feelings without knowing their source. Since people do not like not knowing, they find something in their external reality to blame. That "thing" may be totally unrelated, symbolic, or it may contain a feature that reminds an individual, unconsciously, of the original trauma The individual may then react with what some psychologists term the "as if" affect: responding to a current situation with responses and feelings as if they were responding to a past situation.

Several years ago while doing research on hypnosis, a professor of psychology induced a somnambulistic trance in a subject. The subject was capable of the most profound hypnotic phenomena, including post-hypnotic amnesia. The thrust of this research was to test the theory that, upon carrying out post-hypnotic suggestion, the subject would re-enter the hypnotic state. While in this somnambulistic state, the subject was told that when a clock chimed 10:00 P.M. at that evening's faculty party, she would remove one of her shoes, place it on the dining room table, and put roses into the shoe. Further, it was suggested that she would have no memory of the suggestion, it would appear to be her own idea, and she would feel compelled to finish her task. "A very interesting thing happened on the way to the forum." While she was carrying out the hypnotic suggestion, the professor asked her what she was doing. She replied that her husband had given her a beautiful crystal vase that looked just like her shoe and she had never known what to do with it. She went on to state that it had suddenly dawned on her how to arrange flowers in the vase and she had to try it in her shoe before she forgot. While her explanation appears absurd, she acted as if she believed she was telling the truth. As the professor tried to explain to her how ridiculous her story was, she became anxious, agitated and very defensive. The experiment was terminated due to her extreme anxiety and discomfort.

Now, if we examine the preceding example objectively, we can see a case of post-hypnotic suggestion being carried out without any conscious awareness of the suggestion's source. Further, it shows how desperately the subject searched for a "logical" explanation of her actions and shows the emotional upheaval produced when the subject's explanation was challenged. You, the reader, might be saying, "So what, she was just carrying out a hypnotic suggestion." But, I believe this "hypnotic phenomena" is recreated in all our lives more often than we would believe.

Take the man who walked into the party and "saw" the woman looking at him in a strange way, and responded with rapid heart beat, knots in his stomach, saying to himself, "I know why she's looking at me that way, she hates me." If someone were to challenge his interpretation, he would probably defend it and perhaps become irrational. But, of course, there's no such thing as hypnosis. If my thesis is correct, then the man's response makes as much sense as the woman did with the shoe. Attempting to make sense out of his action and responses will be tedious and probably accomplish very little or less.

CASE 2: FEAR OF HEIGHTS

An example of one hypnotic technique I use along with a partial case history should illustrate how the above fits together. A woman in her 50s had a terrifying fear of heights. She "knew" it was because she had fallen off a five-foot ladder at about eight years old. I told her if the ladder was the cause, then anyone who fell off something five feet high would have the same fear she had. I asked her to close her eyes and see herself climbing a ladder until she felt all the fear and to signal with the first finger of her left hand when she was in touch with that fear. I observed her facial expression, breathing rate, and general appearance. As she evidenced a state of fear, I touched her right arm lightly and said in a slow, even tone: "Hold onto that feeling, and remember when I touch you, you can experience the fear immediately." I then snapped my fingers and said in a faster pace, "Replace that picture with one of beautiful flowers, smell them and feel the pleasure." I observed the changes until she appeared calm and relaxed. I then told her that, when I touched her arm, she would feel the fear and, as if watching a slide projector, she would see scenes clearly going back to the source of that fear and to signal when there. When she signaled, I told her to let go of the uncomfortable feeling as I snapped my fingers and to watch as if seeing someone else until she saw and/or heard something that connected for her and that she wouldn't return to conscious awareness until that connection was made.

After approximately five minutes, she opened her eyes and told the following story: When she was about five, she had a friend who used to climb on boxes and jump off. Her mother caught her one day and told her that one day she was going to break a leg and it would serve her right. Her mother also said that would be a good thing because otherwise she would fall off something high and kill herself. That was a powerful hypnotic suggestion planted beautifully. When she fell off the ladder, it was the same as shining a red light and having the subject raise a hand. From that point on, in her mind, the next fall would kill her and she had no memory of the "suggestion." She then protected herself by developing a phobic reaction to heights. If she avoided heights, she wouldn't die. None of this makes sense except in her mind; there it was real.

The resolution of the problem was accomplished by having her close her eyes and see herself as an army demolition expert. I then touched her arm and told her to "see" all those fears as time bombs and safely blow them all up; that she would then feel the pleasure of the flower and see herself in the garden and to signal when she completed the task. When she signaled, I told her that she would arouse herself bringing back those good feelings. With that, I snapped my fingers to remind her of all those good feelings.

Now, having someone blowing up time bombs doesn't make any more sense than the original hypnotic trauma, except it works. I have observed people evidencing severe anxiety and then a deep sigh of relief when they have finished. Later, many have told me that they were less afraid in general and were responding more comfortably to what had been their problem area. If we again grasp the concept that the problem is really a metaphor, then blowing up time bombs is simply the right tool for the right job, metaphorically speaking.

ROCKET LAUNCHING

If you were to witness the launching of a guided missile, you might be put into a state of awe. You could appreciate the power and sophistication without understanding any of the intricacies—unless you were an expert in the field. You might consider the missile as a vehicle that requires a guidance system and a triggering device. To relate this missile metaphor to our subject, you might consider a past hypnotic-like suggestion as the guidance system, directing behavior (the vehicle) toward a target, and the triggering device as the specific stimulus that triggers the hypnotic suggestion. However, for the vessel to be propelled, it must have fuel, and, in our metaphor, fear is the fuel that keeps the system going.

Underneath all so-called problems, lies that fuel called fear: fear of rejection, fear of dying, fear of falling, fear of not being good enough. Whatever you tag it, it still comes out *fear*. Fear is what makes the field fertile for the "planting" of hypnotic suggestions which result in behavior labeled by some psychiatrists and psychologists as neurotic, psychotic, paranoid, manic-depressive and, in rare cases, normal.

There was a case reported some years back of a young woman who couldn't say "No." She was labeled nymphomaniac. Hypnosis revealed that, as a child, she was expected to obey without question. Her mother would fly into rages if she didn't. One day, she said "No" to her mother. Her mother beat her and she fell back into a stove and was burned by hot water while her mother screamed, "Don't you ever say 'No'!" As a young woman, whenever a man asked her for sex, she would always say "Yes." Without even knowing why, the fear of saying "No" was so great, she carried out the hypnotic suggestion by saying "Yes."

Remember the young man who, every time he gets close to being better than his father, blows it by getting himself fired? He, too, was responding due to his fear and the suggestion of the past. The cast of characters is different but the story (and the monster called fear) is the same.

Fear doesn't have to be rational to affect us powerfully. If you ever had someone pull an "April Fool's" joke that you believed and responded to, or if you have awakened at night hearing creaking in the house and found yourself responding with fear, etc., then you know fear needn't be rational. Fear has been known to block the effects of Novocain in the dental patient. Surgeons are aware that a severely fearful patient is a ripe candidate to require more anesthesia, to die on the table, or to take much longer to recover, etc. Put this emotion which causes so many physical and mental responses together with a post-hypnotic suggestion such as "Don't be better than your father," and you have a potent combination that needn't make sense to affect a person's life in painful ways.

PUTTING THE PIECES TOGETHER

There was a woman who had been institutionalized on three separate occasions. Her history was very interesting. As a little girl, she had watched her mother go crazy and had seen her taken away. Her father would get drunk and yell at her, "You're just like her." That's a pretty strong suggestion and, of course, fear is already there. So, she ends up being institutionalized and dubbed crazy, and there's no such thing as hypnosis. There is very little difference between the above case and the "dynamics" of the subject raising his hand at a red light or at the pull of a tie.

Remember the woman with the shoe? She became fearful when questioned, and then irrational. The more fearful she became, the more irrationally she tried to find a "logical" reason and to defend her behavior. If, for some reason, the sequence were repeated several times, she could develop a conditioned reflex. She might go around trying different arrangements in different shoes. She repeats her behavior to prove she wasn't crazy the first time!

I believe that all learning follows the principles of hypnosis or that all hypnosis follows the principles of learning. You will have to decide for yourself. A child's first experience of reading is through suggestion. For example, the child is shown a picture of a cat. She sees the letters C-A-T, and the teacher repeats "C-A-T spells cat"; see the picture? Sooner or later the child takes the suggestion. It would be just as easy to teach the child that F-Y-Z spells cat. The fear of not belonging, the authority of the teacher, and the repetition of suggestion all combine to produce learning. I am not, for a moment, forgetting positive reinforcement in learning: complimenting the child on his good spelling is important. So is telling the child that children should be seen and not heard, and then complimenting the child for being so quiet. Of course, in the latter example, the child might grow up shy and withdrawn, but the principle remains the principle.

V

Belief Systems

+/– HALLUCINATION

Using traditional hypnosis, you could take a good subject (whatever that is), induce a deep trance (whatever that is), and suggest to the subject that, when he opens his eyes, he will "see" six growling dogs moving toward him in a menacing way. This "good" subject would, upon opening his eyes, respond very strongly to the suggested "metaphor." If he happened to be connected to physiological monitoring devices, they would register his strong responses. While responding to this hypnotically induced metaphor, the subject would evidence anger and defensiveness to any suggestion that the dogs were not really there. His inner belief system tells him that they (the dogs) are real, and that's how he will respond.

Experts in the art of hypnosis would define the above phenomenon as a hypnotically induced positive hallucination—that is, creating something that doesn't exist, to which a subject responds as if it does. Another way of defining the above phenomenon would be to state that, through hypnosis, a belief was temporarily induced (metaphorically) within the subject; that this belief became his inner map of the world, and he responded as if his metaphor were the real world. As long as his "belief system" continues to be operative, he will continue to respond to the "dogs" as if they are real. Bandler and Grinder (1975 a,b) contend that we do not operate on the world directly or immediately, but rather through internal maps (belief systems) of the world, and that the "map is not the territory." The patient—or any individual—who says, "I can't succeed" or "No one has ever loved me" is, in effect, using language to describe his map (inner belief system), but not necessarily the real world, or his real experiences.

44

> Maps, like language, select certain features and ignore others, and like language, maps are cultural expressions of elements significant to society. — Aziz, 1978

I might add that the individual's belief systems are more an expression of elements he has learned to believe are significant. However, what his map has left out may be more important than what he continues to "see."

> Once a person becomes aware of the cultural bias in map-making, he or she can never again take a map as an accurate depiction of the world. Creating a map is like sculpting a statue. What matters is not only what remains in view, but also what has been whittled away.
> — *Human Nature,* Jan. 1979, Vol. 2, no. 1, p. 34

We might state the above proposition in the following manner: we do not respond to reality (whatever reality is). In effect, we respond to and operate upon reality based on our metaphors which become our individual and personal reality.

BELIEFS: GOOD OR BAD

To every transaction between individuals—whether it be between friends, lovers, parent/child, patient/therapist—each person brings with him/her a set of belief systems, or inner maps. I believe that most of these belief systems are effective and enable individuals to obtain their desired goals. However, some of these belief systems may be less than effective, and may lead to painful destinations. The individuals who come into a therapist's office seeking help, also bring with them a whole history, a whole background, a whole set of belief systems. Most of these belief systems are constructive and useful—otherwise those individuals would not have survived long enough to seek help. But, in areas in which they are evidencing pain and dysfunction, their belief system, in that area, is either "the problem" or prevents them from finding the solution. It is as if...once upon a time they were given a map that indicated that San Diego, California was really San Francisco, California. They have spent a great deal of their life trying to prove to everyone that San Diego is San Francisco, and then sneaking up to San Francisco and moving it brick by brick to San Diego to prove that their map was really right. I believe it would be much more helpful to help them make a new map.

It is one of my basic belief systems that individuals have been *hypno-tized* into their metaphoric belief systems, whether those metaphors are graceful and efficacious, or painful and self-limiting. As I have stated earlier, I believe that all learning is a form of hypnosis, and that hypnotic transactions occur between people all the time. The individual who has been hypnotized into "seeing" six growling dogs responds more or less the same way as the person who is "sure" he can't succeed, or who "knows" she will never find anyone to love her, or who "hears" voices telling him to do strange things, etc. Those individuals are "sure" of those things because their belief systems exclude any facts that might prove otherwise. Too often, in my opinion, therapists are prone to accept those painful maps as accurate, and then help their patients to "really get into the feelings."

An individual enters a therapist's office and complains that no one has ever loved him or been kind to him; that everyone has "ripped him off." If the therapist accepts those statements as being true in fact, then I believe that the therapist has experienced being hypnotized by the patient. If you *will now* consider hypnosis as itself a metaphor—that is, hypnosis substitutes one type of awareness for another, one reality for another—then the therapist has been hypnotized into accepting another's reality and awareness as true. In the first place, since that individual has survived to tell his tale, someone, in the past, has been kind to him, fed him, saw to his clothing, etc. What of the kids he played with as a child? Gifts he received in the past? Is he lying? That's one possibility. Another possibility is that his belief systems are such that he has excluded from his conscious awareness anything that might contradict his personal "metaphors." He may even distort his conscious awareness to "fit" his metaphors. The therapist who accepts the patient's "metaphor" as reality is going to find him/herself following the patient's map…and ending up just as lost. But, therapists don't do that…do they? Ridiculous isn't it? Of course, a conservative Republican might insist that all Democrats are horse thieves, but not all horse thieves are Democrats. A liberal Demo-crat might "prove" that all Republicans have "sold out" to big business, but those things are different, aren't they?

In the example of the hypnotically induced metaphor (six growling dogs), "suggestion" keeps the hallucination operative. Where an individ-ual "knows" that everyone hates him, or she will always fail, or whatever the problem may be, his belief systems keep those hallucinations going. We might consider that, at some point in time, someone or something created a metaphor (or hypnotic suggestion) that he interpreted to mean that people hate him, or that he will always fail. During his lifetime, he has, in all probability, experienced someone liking and approving of him, and has no doubt been successful at many things; yet his belief systems produce the hypnotic phenomenon called "negative hallucination" (not seeing or hearing what there is to see or hear), which results in not "seeing" or "hearing" information that conflicts with what he believes. In effect, his belief systems have created an inner map, and he "selects" from the world those signposts that match the map. Just as attempting to convince a hypnotic subject with logic that the "growling dogs" are not real will be met with resistance, so too will attacking his inner belief systems most often be met with the same results…"resistance."

BELIEFS AS MEMORIES

As I stated earlier, we to not respond to, or operate on the world (reality) itself, but rather we operate or respond to the world based on our internal sets of belief systems. To the same "real"-world situation, there can be, and often is, a multitude of responses and beliefs. Two people go to the beach together; one of them smiles and says, "Doesn't that look beautiful? It feels so warm and pleasant. Wow! I just love the beach." The other person responds with, "Gag, it's awful, terrible and dirty. Look at all the sand fleas and the tar on the ground. The heat makes me sticky and smelly. I don't know how you can stand it." Well, the beach is the beach is the beach, and yet…two entirely different, and incompatible, responses. Each individual is responding physiologically, psychologically, and emotionally based on their own belief systems as to the beach. These belief systems stem from their own "memories" (metaphors) as to the meaning of a beach to them, and these "memories" have, in fact, become their own individual reality.

> Memories are thus physical systems in brains whose organization and activities constitute records or representations of the outside world, not in the passive sense of pictures, but as action systems. The representations are accurate to the extent that they allow the organism to represent appropriate actions to the world.
>
> — J.Z. Young, 1978

One might be tempted to say that the beach has become "as if" a hypnotic cue that sets into motion certain specific responses, based on each individual's "memories" as to the beach. But, of course, hypnosis cannot result from a beach, or a memory...can it?

Belief systems, whether graceful and efficacious, or painful and destructive, are formed in a multitude of ways: modeling; learning models; circumstances; traumas; repetition of events; and suggestions; etc. It is my belief, that no matter how they are formed, they affect all of our behaviors in ways that are similar to that of hypnotic phenomena. Whatever the specific causative factors may be, belief systems are at least partially created by, and continue via, the vehicle of suggestion and the examples and parameters set by others.

> We must think of a world image then, as the most comprehensive, most complex synthesis of the myriads of experiences, convictions, and influences, of their interpretations, of the resulting ascription of value and meaning to the objects of perception which an individual can muster. The world image is, in a very concrete and immediate sense, the outcome of communication... (suggestion). It is not a world, but a mosaic of single images which may be interpreted in one way today and differently tomorrow; a pattern of patterns; an interpretation of interpretations; the result of incessant decisions about what may and what may not be included in these meta-interpretations, which themselves are the consequences of past decisions.
>
> — P. Watzlawick, 1978

NEGATIVE BELIEFS

Some people are very much like soft, plush, wall-to-wall carpeting: They tend to keep the imprints of those people who walked on them in the past. Once this happens, these "imprints" (belief systems) supplement, and in many cases, *supplant* so-called reality. When an individual's "mosaic of single images" is continually interpreted in a stereotyped way, he becomes stuck, and his range of choices is limited. If his belief systems tell him that no one likes him, or she always fails, s/he may continue to distort or deny reality to support his "world image." If we again examine a traditional version of hypnosis (hypnotic belief systems) which holds that hypnosis is the communication of ideas and attitudes that take a firm hold on an individual's inner belief systems and then lead that individual to respond to the "implanted suggestions," *we can see more clearly* the relationship between hypnotic phenomena and belief systems. The child who is told to never say no, or that he should not try to be better than his elders, may grow up and act on those suggestions as if they were absolute laws—part of the Ten Commandments. That person "knows" that any violation of such commandments will bring great harm and pain. Now, that's not true in reality, but it is true in that person's inner world—based on his belief systems. That person is operating under the hypnotic phenomenon known as "negative hallucination" that leads him to continually deny external information that would prove that his belief systems are not necessarily accurate. Instead, he continues to be sad, miserable and depressed because his inner belief systems hypnotize him into following the very steps that cause those "suggestions" to bear that sour fruition.

Several years ago, a psychiatrist and I were discussing one of his patients. The psychiatrist was frustrated because he "knew" he could help the patient, "but nothing is happening." He told me he could really help if only his patient was more psychologically astute, more aware, more motivated, and could really understand the "real" purpose of therapy. I replied, "If your patient had all those skills readily available, he sure as hell wouldn't need you! Have you considered working with the patient you have instead of the one you are dreaming about?" The moral of that story is this: If an individual were capable of instantly being the way a therapist wants them to be, they wouldn't be in the therapist's office in the first place. Since that individual has sought help, it is a safe bet to assume that s/he is stuck—at least in some aspect of his/her life. I believe that one of the first and, perhaps, most important tasks at hand, is to discover what keeps that individual from having new choices that would lead to being "unstuck." To make those discoveries, it is my belief that you must examine their belief systems. Once you begin to understand (better yet, recognize) which belief systems are keeping them stuck, you must then begin to work with the individual you have and not the one you may have hallucinated. Using the individual's known—and perhaps, painful—belief systems to lead them to new destinations, is a graceful way to bring about change.

INDUCTION VIA BELIEF SYSTEM

During one of my training seminars, a young psychologist was unhappy because he "couldn't" be hypnotized. He said he had really tried to cooperate, but to no avail; that he could still "hear everything the other person was saying," and that "nothing different had happened." After asking him to sit down in front of the training group, I asked him the following: "I guess you have a pretty good idea of what a person should be saying to you in order to hypnotize you properly, don't you?" He nodded his head yes and said, "I think I do." I replied, "Since we are all here to learn, I would like to know what would need to happen to you to let you know you were in a hypnotic state?" He named several possibilities including arm catalepsy. I emphasized his choice (belief system) by saying, "Do you mean that you believe that arm catalepsy is one way you would know you are in hypnosis?" He replied, "That's right! Absolutely!" I then asked him to do me a "personal" favor and close his eyes, which he did. I then told him that no matter what I said he should ignore my remarks, and instead listen to his own inner voice saying the "proper" words. He nodded his head, and I began saying a few unimportant things, such as "you continue just as you are" and "that's right...even more slowly" (timed to his breathing). After a few more such comments, I said, "and keep on listening to your own inner voice." With that I shut up. After three or four minutes I took his right wrist gently and began to slowly raise his right arm straight out in front of him, and then held it there for about 30 seconds. I then slowly let go. His arm remained where it was, and, after almost five minutes, he opened his eyes. He looked at his still "cataleptic" arm and said, "I'll be damned! I did it!"

The above is an example of using an individual's unique belief system to help him experience change. In this case, the individual's belief systems were used to produce what he wanted, but was failing to achieve: being hypnotized! When he stated that he could still hear the other person's voice and that nothing different had happened, he had used words that described one of his maps, but not necessarily the "real" world. His map told him that he shouldn't hear the "hypnotist's" voice. I, therefore, asked him to hear his *own* voice, and I just stopped talking. In addition, I used what he considered "something different happening"— arm catalepsy—to help him alter his state. Arguing with his belief systems, or continuing to do what had already not worked, only more of it, and better (?) would probably have resulted in a more entrenched individual. You may wish...*now*...to utilize the above example as a guide toward developing some creative new approaches to those patients who are "resistant" and/or "intractable."

If, as I believe, belief systems and the responses that flow from them are almost hypnotic in nature, then using this thing that doesn't exist— hypnosis—to help give individuals a new map, may be, in effect, using what they already know to help them learn and experience something new. Where we fail to do this (use what they know), we may run the risk of encouraging the individual to continue to respond to his old belief systems automatically, and to deny the possibility of change. The individual's response may have become so automated that the source, or original purpose of the response is "lost" from conscious awareness. Young (1978), starting from a different place, and perhaps going somewhere else, said:

All learning action comes essentially from within, as a result of the operation of the programs, part inherited, *part acquired.* These programs co-operate with the signals coming from the sense organs, but even these are not simply imposed on us. What we see and hear is largely the result of our programs of search, some of them following habitual rhythms.

Just as the hypnotic subject will respond to the "six growling dogs" automatically based on the hypnotic "cue" being presented, so too will individuals tend to associate certain external stimuli (cues) with certain stereotyped responses. The external "cue" becomes a symbol, or metaphor, that sets into motion a whole series of responses, as if the individual was carrying out a post-hypnotic suggestion. Young (cited) put that idea this way

...the key to the concept as we are using it is that a symbol is a special sort of signal because it represents the features of the surroundings in such a way that the organism immediately recognizes its significance and acts accordingly.... So the programs of the brain symbolize the environment in the sense that they provide actions that correspond to, or represent it. Some of the programs do this because of heredity and *many of them are built up by the results of experience of the environment recorded in the memory.*

ERICKSON — BELIEFS — METAPHORS

In 1979, I had the pleasure of spending two days with Dr. Milton Erickson at his home in Phoenix, Arizona. At one point, I asked Dr. Erickson the following question: "Would you say that you perceive all presenting symptoms and complaints as being metaphors that contain a story about the 'real' problem, and that your basic approach is to build metaphors that contain a story about the possible solution?" Dr. Erickson's face lit up and, like a little boy finding a surprise, he said, "Exactly!" One of my most important beliefs is that individuals' belief systems are metaphors; that the individual operates and responds metaphorically to the world! It takes metaphoric approaches to help expand each individual's choices.

> After the odyssey through the Magic Theater, the hero in Herman Hesse's *Steppenwolf* laughs out loud as he realizes that reality is nothing but the free choice of one of many doors that are open at all times.
>
> — P. Watzlawick, cited

Once an individual discovers 31 flavors of ice cream, he will find it difficult to insist that there is only vanilla. I hope to point out throughout this book that hypnosis is, itself, a very powerful metaphoric state; that the problem itself is a metaphor based on old belief systems that were produced by conditions that could be labeled hypnosis. It would seem logical, therefore, to grasp and use this powerful tool called hypnosis to help build new, graceful and efficacious metaphors. These new metaphors will then be directed toward new choices and responses to the "real" world. Paul Watzlawick (cited) approaching the same destination from a different direction stated:

> The aim of realistic, responsible therapy can only be increased skill in dealing with life's problems as they arise, but not a problem-free life.

VI

Systems Two

EXCESS BAGGAGE

It is 2:00 a.m. and a man is disembarking from an airplane. He is about to start a vacation in a place he has never been. Excited about his new journey, he makes his way to the baggage area and waits. Within a short time, his baggage arrives. He looks for a porter to help him, but no luck. He takes his baggage and begins making his way through the airport. Only then does he realize that he is carrying excess baggage. As he walks through the winding corridors, the weight of the baggage begins slowing him down. Slowly his excitement fades and is replaced with frustration and fatigue. Each step becomes more painful, and his shoulders cry out from the strain. Soon, each step is agony; he watches his feet, listens to his footsteps, and feels the weight even more. By the time he reaches the airport exit, he is exhausted. What a dumb way to begin a journey. There is, however, one thing that is dumber. If he continues to carry excessive baggage when he knows how dumb that is.

Most therapists, and particularly those who use hypnosis, often make the therapeutic journey a painful one. They do this as a result of the excess and often useless baggage they carry with them. By the time they finish their trip, they and their patients are frustrated and fatigued. The baggage I refer to is that of old belief systems and preconceived ideas as to how people think, experience and communicate. Those of you who have read the fine books written by John Grinder and Richard Bandler (particularly *The Structure of Magic II*) will be familiar with what you will now be reading. However, stick with it, as there will be additional information and subtleties for you to consider. The rest of you may find the information hard to believe. Read on, for you are about to begin a new journey.

One piece of excess baggage we could all do without is the "assumption" that all individuals, more or less, think and process information in a similar fashion. Nothing could be more removed from reality. It is true that we all use our "senses"—eyes, ears, nose, touch, etc.—to "know" the world around us. It is not true that we do so in the same way as everyone else. We not only process information in unique ways, we also express our experiences to others in unique ways. The words we use are, in fact, metaphors for our individual responses and experiences. For people-helpers, or for anyone who is interested in meaningful communication, it is imperative that we know how to translate another's metaphors.

Let us pretend that you and I are walking along a beautiful beach together. We are deep into our individual experience. Our "senses" are taking in the external experience. We smell the salt air, feel the warmth of the sun, and see the beautiful blue sky. Unconsciously, each of us is processing all of this input. This processing will be based on our past experiences, belief systems, expectations and values as to a beach. We each will become consciously aware of all or a portion of our processing. If we sit down together to discuss our experience, we each will find certain words coming into our mind that describes the experience for ourselves. We each may "assume" that the other has the same words and experienced the same things. Of such "assumptions" rotten communications are born.

CONSCIOUS OUTPUT SYSTEM

I would like you to consider the words we use to communicate our internal experiences to another person as our *conscious output system*: that is, how we attempt to communicate our experiences to another after we have become "aware" of the experiences. Most of us tend to "assume" that our output system is the same as everyone else's. Experts in the field of language, and those who specialize in brain hemispherics, have "discovered" that this is not the case. By the time an individual is about eleven or twelve years old, they have developed a *preferred* output system. This system indicates which part of the individual's experiences he tends to make most important—at least consciously. These "output" systems come in three varieties: Visual—Kinesthetic—Auditory. It has been estimated that 40% of the population, at least in the United States, tend to prefer a visual system for expressing their experiences to another. These individuals tend to use highly visual words such as, "I *see* what you mean," "That *looks* good to me," "I am still not *clear* as to output systems. Could you *show* me an example?"

There is a second 40% of the population that tends to prefer a kinesthetic "output" system in communication to others. They tend to use such phrases as, "This is *hard* for me to *grasp,*" "I want to get a *handle* on it," "Hey! It is starting to *fall* into place." In short, these individuals tend to feel it is important to put out information in a firm and solid manner so you can get a hold of it. Last, but not least, there is another 20% who tend to prefer an auditory "output" system. These individuals tend to use many words so as to insure understanding. In addition, they use phrases such as, "That *sounds* all right to me," "It is starting to *ring a bell,*" "I want to *buzz* you with an idea. Let me know if it *sounds* exactly right."

OUTPUT SYSTEM: THE BEACH

Let us return to the beach for a few moments. If we were to ask a "visual" individual what s/he liked about the beach, we might hear the following: "I like watching the waves and the beautiful sky. You can see the people really having a good time, and besides, when I get a tan, I look good." If we asked the same question of a "kinesthetic" person, s/he might say, "I really enjoy the warmth. I can feel the tension drop away. It really makes me feel loose and tingly all over." An auditory might respond: "I really like the sound of the waves crashing down. It is much quieter, and I can really hear myself think."

On the other hand, a "visual" might say, "I really love looking at the beach, and the beautiful blue water. It makes me feel good." While s/he ended with a "kinesthetic" phrase, s/he arrived there via a visual path. A "kinesthetic" might say, "I really loosen up when I come to the beach. I feel calm and can take time to see what is going on." S/he ended with a visual statement, but moved firmly through "kinesthetic" to get there. The "Auditory" individual could say, "It is so quiet at the beach. I have time to sound out new ideas. I can look at the people and feel calm."

At this point, some of you may be a bit incredulous. You may be thinking, "I use *all* those systems." That is true...and not true...at the same time. A right-handed person uses his/her left hand, but tends to rely on the right hand more often than the left.

Individuals who tend to be highly visual also use kinesthetic and auditory phrases. However, if you pay *attention,* you will begin to *see clearly* that they *paint* verbal *pictures.* They will *show you* what they want you to *see.* If you were to ask a visual person to "put a handle" on something, they will tend to get a picture of a handle. They will then wait for you to tell them where to put "it" (careful...).

An individual who happens to be highly kinesthetic will also use visual and auditory phases. When you really *get in touch* with what they are doing, you will find that they are *trying* to give you their *feeling* for things. They would like you to really *get a hold* of what they are *giving you.*

The auditory person can fool you. My experience has been that they have a very highly developed second system. That second system may be either visual or kinesthetic. Again, if you really listen, you will hear what their preferred system is. They will tend to use *many words* to describe their feelings (kinesthetic) or to make a picture.

In any case, if you will get rid of the excessive baggage of a closed mind, I believe you will have an exciting new journey. By "paying attention" and "tuning in" and "getting a hold of things," you will discover the individual's preferred system. You may even enjoy finding what *your* "output" system is.

At this point, I would like to recommend a little caution. It has been represented by many "systems" experts that a visual person is always primarily visual, a kinesthetic remains kinesthetic, and once an auditory, always an auditory. I do not agree with that conclusion. My experience has been that an individual may be primarily kinesthetic in one set of experiences and circumstances, visual in another set of circumstances and experiences, and auditory in other experiences and circumstances. I also believe that where the individual functions gracefully, s/he will tend to utilize all systems more or less equally—with one system a little more equal. Conversely, I believe that you will find a different story in the areas of dysfunction. In those areas, as a general rule, you will find that the individual is more or less "stuck" on one system. Think *now,* of the typical "depressed" patient. In almost all cases they will be not only stuck in kinesthetic, but in a *painful* kinesthetic system. You, the reader, might be wondering what does all of "this" have to do with hypnosis and therapy? Relax, feel comfortable, begin to see the picture, and listen. We are moving toward those areas now.

HEAR THE FEELING OF THE PICTURE

The way in which we experience something visually is entirely different from the experience of feeling "it," which is different from the experience of hearing it. Think of each one of the conscious output systems as a "person" within us. Where these "persons" are working in partnership, we will tend to have more than enough choices available to us. If, however, we are only using one of the "partners"—e.g., the auditory system—to solve a problem, and that "partner" does not have the answer, we may be in trouble. We may continue to follow our own footsteps in a continuous circle.

Since it is easier to describe a telephone when you are holding one than it is to describe one when you have never experienced a telephone, I would like to paint a picture for those who need to see. For those who are still trying to grasp it, let me give you something to hold on to. Of course, those of you who need to hear it, can read the words. If we were to take the experience of summer and describe it visually, we might say, "I love seeing the blue skies, the beautiful green trees, all the bright colors of the flowers." If we were then to describe the feelings of summer, we could talk about "the warm sun, the feeling of a soft summer breeze, the feelings of peace and tranquility." That would be a very different description of summer than the first one. If we went on to describe the sounds of summer, we could say, "I like the sounds of the ocean, the sounds of birds singing, and the rustling sound the trees make in a summer breeze." That is a third way of describing the experience of summer. Each one of those ways is, in and of itself, incomplete and impoverished. None of those descriptions would be as complete as a description that includes all three: "Ah, I love summer. It feels so warm and relaxing. I see so many bright colors of the flowers, and the sky is beautiful. I love the sounds of summer, too. Birds singing, and at the beach, the sound of the ocean is so soothing." Now, we have a multisensory "Gestalt" description of summer. Each one of our "partners"—or systems—has a unique way of experiencing the world around us. Because of each "partner's" specialization, each system has a different way of responding, and of solving problems.

At my Clinical Hypnosis: Innovative Technique® seminars, I attempt to "show" people just how different our responses can be, depending on our "systems." I will pick three people from the group, having discovered what their preferred system is. I end up with one of each, unless I goof. I ask the "visual" to hold out his right hand. I then ask him to get the feeling of warmth in "that" hand. Many are unable to accomplish that task at all. Some do so, but with observable effort. I will then ask him to look up and get a clear picture of the sun on a warm day. When he signals (nods his head) that he has done so, I say, "Now, reach up with your hand and see the sun warming your hand. When you feel the warmth lower your hand." Usually, within ten seconds, he will lower his hand and acknowledge that he feels the warmth.

I then ask the "kinesthetic" to look up and get a clear picture of the sun. She will have a great deal of difficulty, and, in most cases, will be unable to "get the picture." I will then instruct her as follows: "I would like you to hold your right hand out in front of you, about waist high. Now, I would like you to remember what a warm, moist hand feels like. When you have that feeling in that hand, just nod." When she nods (usually within a few seconds), I then say, "Now, slowly lift that hand straight up, taking all those warm feelings with it. When you get it up, build a firm picture of the warm sun that will match the feelings." Within seconds she will nod.

With the "auditory," I will attempt to ascertain which system is *not* their second system. For our example, let us assume his second system is kinesthetic. I will ask him to get a picture, just as with the visual. He will have great difficulty. I will then tell him, "I would like you to remember the sound the waves make as they crash down." When he nods, I continue: "Now, as you hear the waves, I want you to remember the warmth of the sand and see yourself putting that hand into the sand. When you feel the warmth in your hand, slowly raise that hand and build a picture of the sun." He, too, will find himself successful. Each one ends up being successful, but each one takes a different road.

You could stop now, and take a small break. During that break, you could begin to wonder how the above examples might have important ramifications for the areas of communication, therapy and hypnosis.

CASE 3: SYSTEMS FOR INDUCTION

Now that you have had a "wondering" break, I would like to give you an example from my clinical practice. A colleague of mine, a physician, asked me to consult with a patient. This patient was suffering intractable pain throughout his back. He had been hospitalized for a series of tests. The tests had revealed that he had terminal cancer, but he had not been informed of the findings at that point. When I met with the patient, he made statements such as, "It hurts. I feel torn up by the pain. I can't stand up to the pain much longer." By his output systems (words), I knew he was, at least in his present experience, kinesthetic. I asked him what he, in the past, had found peaceful and relaxing. "Sailing," he replied, and his face relaxed slightly. I then asked him what he liked about sailing. His reply was most informative. "I like the sound the boat makes going through the water, and the rippling sound the sails make when you have a good wind." With those brief remarks, he had told me what system he used to reach the feelings of relaxation and peacefulness. I asked him to close his eyes and remember the sound of rain hitting a window. After a few moments, I asked him to remember the sound of crackling fire. When I could see the signs of relaxation (deeper breathing, facial muscles relaxing), I asked him to "see" the flames as he listened to the sounds of the warm relaxing fire. I then said, "As you begin to feel the peaceful warmth of the fire, your whole body knows how to remember all the pleasure. Then you might want to see yourself sailing." There was now evidence of deep relaxation. After several more requests by me for auditory memories leading to kinesthetic experiences, he had entered hypnosis.

CASE 3: SYSTEMS — PAIN REDUCTION

The technique described above is an updated version of a very old hypnotic technique. "Old time" hypnotists knew that if you helped an individual to use their "imagining," they could control or eliminate pain. They were utilizing systems, without knowing what it is they really knew. I would like to give you the basic tools that will help you to accomplish the same end.

Where you have an individual who is in physical pain, whether from an accident or illness, that person will be very much into their kinesthetic system. The goal is to help them move into another system; e.g., visual. This will help them to actually utilize a different area of the brain from the part that controls pain. When you have accomplished that switch, their perception of pain drops while their perception of comfort increases. To put it to you in another way: You are helping them to use a different system for the "expression" of their problem (pain). One way of producing that result is to ask the "pain patient" to make a "picture" of what the pain would look like. For example, a woman was complaining of a severe headache in my office. She said that it was so bad that she didn't think we could continue our session. I asked her to close her eyes, and see what color her headache was. She looked at me as if I was crazy. Of course, she was right. I just get paid well for it. Finally, she shrugged her shoulders and closed her eyes. After a short time, she informed me that she did have a picture of colors, and that "it seems to be bright reds and oranges." I then instructed her to listen to the steady sound of her breathing, and with each exhalation, she would breathe more and more of those colors out of her system. She was told to continue until she could see it "all" across the room, as if a painting hanging on the wall. It was several minutes before she signaled that the picture was on the wall. I asked her to see someone walking into the room, taking the picture off the wall, and to hear that person's footsteps as he walked out of the room. In less than five minutes she terminated the hypnotic state that she had spontaneously achieved, with the headache gone.

From what you have just read, I know that you can see and grasp firmly the concept that each system has a different way of "expressing" itself. If an individual is unable to "solve" a problem—pain in the above example—you, as a people-helper, can help him/her utilize a different system. In the areas of "emotional pain," perhaps "looking" in a new way may help him/her to see a solution. Perhaps "listening" or "grasping" something new might do the trick. Changing the "pain patient's" kinesthetic system to a visual one will almost always do the trick. I have used that method with severe burn patients, cancer patients, and for surgeries in which anesthesia could not be used. You could...*TRY IT YOURSELF.* You may be very pleased.

SYSTEM MISMATCH: EXERCISE

Recently, while dining at a restaurant, I overheard a conversation between a well-known actress and her two companions, one of whom was evidently her producer. She was describing her last few days as "being uptight." She made statements such as, "I've really been tied up in knots; the stress of our shooting schedule is crushing me; I finally had a good night's sleep; I just floated off and woke up this morning feeling lighter; I have decided to stay loose." The producer listened politely and then responded, "You should see the rushes. You look great. We have a good product and when they see it they will be impressed." As the producer talked, the actress began to look annoyed and then bored, and then, totally uninterested. As soon as the producer finished, she turned to her other companion and began talking with animation. She hardly said two words to the producer from that point on. Here was a beautiful example of how not to communicate. If I had not been aware of the subject of their conversation, it would have sounded like two disjointed and separate conversations.

Becoming aware of the output system of the people around you may be the beginning of a very exciting adventure. To help you to take that trip, I would like to give you an exercise that you can choose to go out and enjoy doing, or you can just do it and then choose to enjoy it. You can even choose not to choose to do it. That is also your choice. In public places such as restaurants, listen to and watch the people around you. Pay attention to the fact that some people will paint vivid pictures with their words. If they are describing a trip to the mountains, they may use words that describe what the mountains looked like. As they talk, some may even paint a picture by the movement of their hands. Another person may describe the same subject by the feelings of the experience. "I felt so calm and relaxed in the mountains, and the soft mountain breeze really felt good." As they talk, their hand gestures will be that of "getting in touch" with something; contact to their own body; touching their chest areas; contact with the other person. The auditory will tend to talk about how the mountains sound to him. They may use many words to describe the experience in detail. Even when they are describing the feelings or something visual, they will tend to use many words. Some people may fool you at first. As you really tune in, you will grasp their system more easily and see clearly how different those systems are. Keep in mind that each system is important and that no system is "better" than another, and that all of the systems exist within us.

After you have practiced listening to the people around you, and are becoming comfortable in recognizing their (preferred) output system, you are ready for the next step. You can now begin to take a more *active* role in discovering their preferred output system. In general conversations, you can begin to ask neutral questions, such as, "What does comfort mean to you?" or "What did you enjoy most on your vacation?" To questions phrased in that manner, a kinesthetic might reply, "I feel loose, relaxed, without pressure," or "It really felt good to get away. I could feel the everyday stress fall away." A visual, in responding to the question about comfort, might say something like, "I see myself in a beautiful piece where the sky is blue, and everything looks peaceful." To the question about their vacation, the visual might respond, "Wow! The scenery was great. There was so much to see." In any case, you will be pleasantly surprised to discover the differences. Be careful when you are asking these questions, however. If you ask someone, "Can you describe what the mountains looked like to you?" you will, in most cases, get a "visual" answer. Through "demand characteristics" you are asking them to switch to a visual system. "How did you feel on your vacation" demands a kinesthetic response. Most individuals, unless they are under stress, are flexible enough to "switch."

Let us suppose a person enters a therapist's office and says that they are suffering from depression. S/he goes on to say that s/he is being crushed by his/her feelings, and is really feeling down. S/he is, at that moment in his/her life, stuck in the kinesthetic system. S/he is in pain, which is a kinesthetic experience. As long as s/he continues to stay in that system, the problem will remain. If the kinesthetic system contained choices s/he could easily use to be more comfortable, I believe s/he would have made that choice. As you begin to help that person step back and look at what is going on in his/her life, you are helping him/her to "switch" systems. This often leads to "seeing" different choices. Switching an individual from their conscious output system will often result in that state that does not exist...hypnosis. In addition, it helps the individual "use" another part of their brain from the part that is causing the "problem." In effect, you help them to break their "mind set," and enable them to call upon another "partner," or system, for the solving of their problem.

CASE 4: SYSTEMS — DEPRESSION

A woman entered my office in what I could best describe as a "crushed" state. She sat slumped in a chair, and used one kinesthetic phrase after another to describe the state of her life and being. Using kinesthetic phrases, I asked her to really get in touch with those feelings, and to hold them. She was instructed to close her eyes and to really feel all the feelings, with particular effort to be made experiencing her physical sensations. This part of the procedure began a process of directing her attention away from her emotional state to that of her physical state. Next, she was told to feel her mind beginning to build a clear picture of what all those feelings would look like. I said, "The picture you get may be colors, or some situation, it may look sensible or nonsensical."

Within a few minutes, her breathing rate had deepened and her general demeanor was much improved. Several minutes later she began to laugh, and stated, "I have a picture but it doesn't make any sense. In fact it looks ridiculous." I said, "You now have several choices as to how to deal with that picture"—an implied suggestion that there were options in reaching a new solution. "You can either remember the sound of the wind and see the picture being blown further and further away until you can see a beautiful sky. In that clear sky is a bright warm sun, and you can soon feel all that warmth and comfort." This last statement offered her the option of moving back to her kinesthetic system, but now in a pleasurable way. This would result in a basic restructuring of her kinesthetic experience. "Another choice you have is to question some object or person in your picture. If you do so, listen first to the sound of that voice, and then the words, until it is clear to you."

She chose the second method, and within five minutes she opened her eyes with a start. She informed me that she now knew what was bothering her. I asked her to again close her eyes, which she did. I then said, "I would like you to let your creative unconscious mind produce a new picture. This picture will be from some time in your past when you felt stuck in a similar situation, but where you had found a solution. I would like you to then watch that part of you as she updates that solution to fit your present situation until it looks just right. Then wait until what you see feels good and strong, and you experience those feelings now." It was nearly ten minutes more before she opened her eyes. She smiled and said, "I'm not sure what happened, but I feel very good." I then asked her to practice changing any uncomfortable feelings into pictures, just as she had done in my office. Two days later her husband called. He told me that his wife was happier and more relaxed than he had seen her in months, and that "she even looks and acts younger." The procedure as described was not a cure, but it was a giant step in the direction of new choices.

SYSTEMS: RAPPORT

An important and practicable application of the use of output systems concerns the establishment of rapport. Meeting someone in "their system" establishes rapport almost instantly, and improves rapport with those people you are now interacting with. In addition, being able to communicate in another's system can help you to quickly make a connection to the so-called emergency patient. The following example will make those points clearly.

A young man had been referred to three different therapists by his physician. He had been given three names because he was doubtful that he could find a therapist who could help. The young man had been in a deep depression for several months, and his physician considered him suicidal. He had been in therapy two years prior to his present "outbreak," but with little success.

At this point, he was feeling totally hopeless. Mine was one of the three names he had been given. When he called me, I listened carefully to the way he expressed himself. Some of the statements he made were, "I feel crushed by my problems; I don't know if I can stand up to it much longer; I know I'm going to collapse soon." To his (kinesthetic) statements, I responded, "It must be rough trying to carry that burden yourself. You must get really down from the struggle. I would like you to reach down and grasp just enough strength to get in to my office. I really feel that if we get together and tackle this problem, we will be able to pound out a solution. Once you get a handle on things, the weight will fall away." He responded, "Thank God! I finally found somebody who understands my problem." Now, I had no idea what his "real" problem was. I knew that he was stuck in one system, at least as to his present problem. I needed to meet him in that system before I could even begin to lead him out. Rapport was established, on the phone, within a few minutes. He kept his appointment, and within a few sessions he was beginning to "look" for new solutions, and was beginning to "see" things that needed to be "clarified."

Let us recap together. What you have been reading describes the *conscious output system*: How an individual communicates in their own conscious mind (internal dialogue) as well as to the listener, what their present experience is. I hope you have a clear picture as to what the visual system is. I have made every effort to paint a clear picture for you. I also want you to grasp the concept of the kinesthetic system. I feel confident that you will get comfortable with it. For those of you who are auditory, you could read all the words again until they sound right and ring true. Keep in mind also, that in helping someone to use all their systems, you help them to discover new choices. Within each system is information that may include a solution: information they may have heard, something they may have seen, or a time they responded with different feelings in a similar situation.

Among all of their systems there is an answer. However, where an individual is only relying on one system and is stuck, they are, in effect, excluding from their conscious awareness at least two-thirds of their history and experiences. If that is the case, it is not surprising that they are in pain. What is surprising is how well they have done in spite of their self-imposed handicap.

VII

GIGO

Now that you have mastered, and are comfortable with, output systems, you are ready to continue your journey. We will now move into the area of internal systems, processes and programs. This part of your journey will help you to understand just how an individual generates the *internal experiences* that lead to the conscious output. Before we actually begin, we need to take a side trip to a computer room.

As you enter the computer room, you may be overwhelmed by the apparent complexity of the computer itself. If you will, think of that computer as a sophisticated shovel: in short, a tool to be directed by you. The computer has been designed with certain built-in characteristics and capabilities. All it does is make calculations at an incredibly rapid rate. However, if the "programmer" creates a poor program, then what comes out will be "garbage." This process is also known as "GIGO," which is computer-eze for "garbage in/garbage out." Even where the program that is "punched in" is OK, you still may get garbage out when the computer's internal programs (such as its "start-up" program or operating system) are not operating properly.

If you were to consider the computer's communications—e.g., a visual display—as its output system, you could then consider the programmer's data and information as the system's input. You could go one step further and consider its built-in capacity and programs as a sort of "unseen" and "unknown" system that is, in fact, central to the computer's "functioning and well-being." You may want to draw a parallel between the way people process their programs and what you have been reading. If so, good. Read on and the parallels will become even more clear, and important.

UNCONSCIOUS INPUT SYSTEM

As you have already discovered, the way an individual communicates with words indicates what their *conscious output system* is. What may be even more important is the "programs" they use to generate their conscious experience. I term this system the *unconscious input system.* "Unconscious," because, in the majority of situations, the individual is not consciously aware of what they are doing. "Input," because it is as if it is a "program" for the processing of their experiences. Where an individual is responding to a "here-and-now" experience with here-and-now responses, his/her unconscious input system plays but a small part. However, if individuals always responded in a "here-and-now" manner, they would probably have little or no need to be therapized. In the areas of their "dysfunction," it is a safe bet that they are responding to something other than the "here-and-now." Where their input system is a GIGO system, what comes out will draw flies.

Let us digress for a moment. Earlier I referred to a walk along the beach. In such a situation, most of us would be responding to the beach. Our senses and responses would not only be engaged in the experience of the beach, we would also be pretty much conscious of the majority of our experience. If someone were to ask you to remember the first time you went to a beach, you would then go to your unconscious input system: that is, you would use a certain "program" for finding that memory within you. A trained observer could know by just what method you generated that memory. This observer would know your "program" by what you did with your eyes. In 1969, a gentleman by the name of Bakan discovered a relationship between eye movement and hemispheric recall. His work, along with the works of many others, has established specific relationships between eye position and movement, and the type of "recall" the individual is experiencing. This "recall" may be visual, kinesthetic, auditory, or combinations of all three. Where the individual's unconscious input (recall) system is GIGO, then s/he will experience a lot of garbage.

For example, what if we were to ask a friend how he was going to do on a job interview? As he begins to respond, he makes a "picture" out of his past. Let us assume that this picture is one in which he made a fool of himself at a grade school recital. Let us further assume that this picture is mainly unconscious. There is a very good chance that he will experience some bad feelings. He will probably assume that the prospect of the interview is causing them. He may then say, "I am really scared. I always screw up at interviews." If you could help him become aware of the "real" source of his fear, you could help him to have a new choice. If he is not so helped, he will continue to hypnotize himself into responding to interviews "as if" he was a kid in grade school, and he will probably have amnesia for the picture he is "really" seeing. At this point you might be thinking, "Sounds great! But how do I go about it?" As you continue your journey, you will discover the how of it.

THE EYES HAVE IT

For you to understand another's unconscious (input) system, you must first learn what different eye movements and positions mean. I would like you to imagine a face looking at you, or if it will help, draw a face on a piece of paper. Next, I want you to pretend that the whole world is right-handed/left-hemispheric dominant. Now, of course, that is not even close to true; we will explore the variations as we continue. Now, go back to the imagined face or the one you have drawn. I would like you to "see" the eyes turning up to that "person's" left—your right, as you look at them.

Where an individual is looking up to their left, s/he is triggering that part of the brain in which *PAST VISUAL* memories are stored. Another way of stating that would be: S/he is seeing something s/he has seen in his/her history. When that individual looks up to the right—your left as you look at them—they are *CONSTRUCTING VISUAL* images: that is, s/he is making a picture of a new idea, understanding or something they have never seen before. For example, if you were to ask someone to get a clear picture of an elephant, they would, in the vast majority of cases, look up to their left. After they "got the picture" (which could be within a split second), they would then look back at you.

In many cases, they would also nod their head slightly. If you then asked him/her to get a clear picture of the colors red and orange, they would again look up to the left. If you then asked them to get a clear picture of a red and orange polka-dotted elephant, they would look up to the right. (They might first look briefly up to the left to "recall" each piece, before looking to the right.) S/he would look up to the right because, hopefully, they have not experienced one of those in their real world of the past. (If they have, please give them my card.)

Be aware and forewarned! Some, and perhaps most individuals, will make it easy for you. Their eye movements will be very pronounced. A few individuals will have eye movements that are very quick and minimal. Practice... You will "see" it almost intuitively.

When, in response to a question or in any other situation, an individual looks down to their left—your right as you look at them—they are, at that moment, into their internal *AUDITORY SYSTEM*. In effect, they are having an internal dialogue. They may be rehearsing what they are about to say, or re-hearing a past conversation or any previous auditory experience. Another possibility is that they are "analyzing" something they have heard or wish to say.

When an individual looks down to their right—your left as you look at them—s/he is recalling *PAST KINESTHETIC EXPERIENCES*. As you observe that person, you will often see evidence of their kinesthetic experience: facial color changes; bottom lip becoming fuller; changes in breathing rate. As a general rule, when someone is experiencing a present kinesthetic experience, s/he will tend to look in the general direction of the listener and make physical contact to their own body. It is when that individual is attempting to recall a past experience of "feelings" that the individual will look down to their right.

PREFERRED UNCONSCIOUS SYSTEM

In our discussion of conscious output systems, I attempted to point out that, while we use all systems, we also tend to have one system that is preferred. This is also the general rule for our unconscious input system. (As you read on, you will find that the exceptions are as frequent as the rule.) As you begin to observe the people around you, I am confident that you will "see" that each individual tends to utilize one unconscious system far more than the others. Some individuals will, in the vast majority of situations, make reference to their unconscious visual system. When asked a question, or when they are trying to recover information, they will invariably move their eyes up, usually to their left. This movement indicates that they are finding "the picture." Some individuals will almost always move their eyes down right when searching for past information. In effect, they are trying to grab hold of, and get the feeling of the information. A few individuals will look first down to their left in searching for information, or recalling a past experience. This tells you that they are using words as their "program" for recall.

By paying attention to eye movements, you, as a communicator, as a people-helper, and as a person who cares, will gain a great deal of information. You will know just how an individual is, at that moment in time, processing information or experiences at an unconscious level. You will "see" just what their "program" is. With this information, you will be able to communicate in a very powerful way. You can begin to communicate to that person at both the conscious and unconscious level. Imagine that you are having a conversation with an individual. If that person's conscious output system is visual, and s/he is referencing to her visual unconscious (input) system, then you need to "talk visually," both with your words and eye movements. If you move your eyes up for a split second before you speak and as you finish, you will have communicated to that person's unconscious system. You eye movements signal that you "understand" how that person is generating their experience at that moment in time. (In the last section on systems, I will give examples of communication to be used where the individual output system and input system are mixed: e.g., the output system is kinesthetic while the input system is visual.)

PATTERN VARIATIONS

There are several subtleties and variations that you will want to become aware of. For example, where an individual is planing his/her eyes back and forth on a more or less mid-line, s/he is experiencing an internal (auditory) argument with him/herself. In many instances, they are also generating very rapid, and often confusing, visual images. This "program" can occur in any individual from time to time, but is most often seen where the individual is under extreme stress. In fact, severely dysfunctioning individuals often evidence this pattern. It can be very painful, and is usually a true GIGO program.

Another variation is that of the "straight ahead" visualizer. This is a "program" where the individual appears to be looking at the listener, but is, instead, generating internal visual experiences. Often, such an individual is nearly oblivious to the people and events that are occurring in the world around at that moment. There are two main clues for spotting this program: Staring without blinking, and pupillary dilation. If you believe that an individual is engaged in this pattern, you can test to see if you are correct. You might hold your hand out and say, "What color rose am I holding?" If the individual looks puzzled or confused, s/he was probably not "picturing" straight ahead. On the other hand, if s/he continues to stare, and gives you an answer—e.g., "It's red"—you have guessed right. If you were to then reach out and "hand" him/her that rose, s/he might even take "it." You could even suggest that s/he close her eyes and continue to hold and look at the rose. If you do so, be prepared to be somewhat alone. S/he will probably enter into hypnosis. I could be incorrect. S/he may already be into the hypnotic state.

There is one other important variation you need to consider for the auditory/visual pattern. Where an individual seems to be "looking right through you," s/he is really auditorializing and making a picture of what s/he is saying. In effect, s/he does not even see you, the listener. Instead, s/he has literally altered consciousness; is looking in the distance at an imaginary blackboard; talking internally and picturing either the words, or the scenes that match the words. Most individuals find this pattern disconcerting when directed at them. It is probably the single most misunderstood of all patterns. When a man uses this pattern with a woman, she will often feel as if he is "undressing" her. In reality, he hardly knows she is there. Where it is a woman using this pattern with a man, he will often feel as if "she acted as if I was nothing." Again, she is so into her own process, she's unaware of the world around her. I believe that this pattern always results in a form of "self-hypnosis." If, while someone is using this pattern, you make a sudden move (e.g., raise your arm high) or make a sudden noise (e.g., snap your fingers), you will see them almost jump. They will look confused and startled. It will be almost as if they were brought out of a "trance" too quickly. Often, that person will evidence amnesia for what had transpired just prior to their "awakening."

LEFT – RIGHT – LEFT

Now, we can consider all of those people who are not right-handed, left-hemisphere dominant. Where the individual is left-handed, it is an easy transition. Just reverse the meaning of eye movements. If a left-hander looks up to his right, he is generating past visual. If he looks up to his left, he is constructing new pictures. Eyes down right equals auditory, while eyes down left indicates kinesthetic memories. The variations mentioned above have the same general meaning regardless of left/right-hemispheric dominance.

Sounds and looks simple, does it not? Well, it is and it is not. There is a category of individuals that I term "cross-brain dominant." These are individuals who may be right-handed, while they are right-brain dominant as if they were left-handed. On the other hand (pun intended), they may be left-handed and left-brain dominant as if they were right-handed. When in doubt as to how a person is organized at the unconscious level, ask questions. For example, you might ask questions that require past visual recall: What color was your first car? What style was the first house you lived in? Pay attention to where the individual puts his eyes. If he looks up to the right for past information, forget what "hand" he is. His hemispheric dominance will tell you from where he is getting his experience. His handedness will only tell you with which hand he will sign his name, and for our purposes, that is not too terribly important.

SYSTEM MYTHS

I am now going to go out on a limb. I hope that you will refrain from sawing it off while I am perched upon it. If you do saw it off, make sure there is a nice soft pillow for me to land on.

There are some "facts" that most experts on systems agree upon. I find myself in total disagreement with a few of these "facts." The first fact is: where the individual's unconscious (input) system is different from their conscious (output) system, that individual is incongruent. I believe that an individual can have so-called "mixed" systems and still be very congruent. In my opinion, it is the way they *use* their mixed system in the real world that determines whether there is a problem or not. Where the individual functions well, and has the ability to make choices, then their mixed system is merely their unique program. It is only where their mixed system produces pain and lack of choices that I would label their mixed systems GIGO.

The next fact I would like to dispute is that of the preferred input system. (Some systems people call this the "lead" system). The general view is that individuals almost always have a specific preferred unconscious system. If their preferred unconscious system is visual, they will almost always move their eyes up to the visual area; and similarly if their preferred system is either auditory or kinesthetic. During my many years of experience, I have found that the preferred unconscious input system often changes. While I agree that there *is* a preferred unconscious system, I also believe that we change our preferred unconscious system depending on the circumstances and our internal "memories." In addition, an individual may have one preferred unconscious system in, let us say, a *pleasant* experience, while that system may be entirely different in a *painful* situation. In short, they may have two different programs depending on the emotional content of their experiences.

Example: An individual is telling you about a pleasant experience. Their output system is kinesthetic, while their input system (eye movements) is visual. They then begin to discuss an unpleasant and painful experience. Their output system stays the same, while their input changes to auditory. This type of switching can take place within all the systems (K—A—V) and in any combination. In the last section on systems, I will make some recommendations as to how to deal with these "switching" systems, and what the switch itself might indicate.

OUT OF CONSCIOUS SYSTEM

Most system experts contend that the way an individual speaks (conscious output), eye movements (unconscious input), and so-called "body language" add up to all of the individual's communication systems. I believe that there exists one more system: the *Out of Conscious Unconscious System* (out of conscious system). This system, at first, sounds complicated. As you become comfortable with it, you will discover that not only is it easy to understand, it may also be the key to a successful therapeutic outcome.

If we were to refer back to the analogy of a computer, you will recall I made mention of a computer's operating system. Generally, this system is "unseen and unheard." The out of conscious system "performs" in the same way. If an individual is using words such as, "I see what you mean," "That looks clear to me," "I enjoy seeing a blue sky and seeing beautiful scenery," that person is, at that moment, utilizing a visual output system. If, at the same time, they are using visual terms and are also moving their eyes up left and right, you would know that, at that moment, their unconscious input system was also visual. If you were to ask that person if s/he was aware that s/he was making pictures in their mind, and they confirmed that fact, then you would know that their unconscious system is one that they can bring into consciousness without difficulty.

There are many individuals, however, who will claim that they are not making pictures, or who will claim that "I can't visualize." In realty, that cannot be true. In their personal realty, it is true for them. What that person is really saying is: "I am unable to become consciously aware of the images my mind is producing at this moment in time." In point of fact, they *are* generating pictures, or that person would not know what a chair is, or where they parked their car, but s/he is blocked as to conscious awareness of the internal pictures. Therefore, their visual system is, in this example, an *Out of Conscious Unconscious System.* In short, any system (K—A—V) that an individual is unable to bring into awareness, or that they are unaware of, is their out of conscious system. In the areas of dysfunction and pain, the out of conscious system may prevent the individual from having choices as to change.

BLOCKED SYSTEMS: EXAMPLES

If you or I were to visually recall an unpleasant experience from our past, we would probably begin to experience some unpleasant feelings. You might pause now...and remember some past trauma; see it as clearly as possible...and now become aware of feelings that match what you are "seeing." Since you are aware of the connection between what you are "seeing" and what you are "feeling," you have several choices that will change your feelings. You could stop the pictures, or change them to something that is pleasurable, or remind yourself that it is in the past and you survived it. But the individual who is seeing something painful, without the ability to "know" that they are "seeing" it, has a painful problem. That person will become aware of their painful feelings, but will have no idea from whence they come. Without that awareness, s/he has little or no control over what s/he will continue to experience consciously!

The individual whose visual system is out of conscious, or who claims that they cannot get visual images, is someone who, during some period of their life, was forced to, or accidentally saw things that looked very scary and caused a great deal of pain. To protect themselves from that pain, they brought down a mental curtain over those (visual) memories, and, in effect, produced amnesia for those events—at least in the visual experience. Those pictures from the past are going on internally, but that person is afraid to see them. To avoid looking at these painful images, they block out "seeing" any pictures.

Another example of the Out of Conscious Unconscious System would be that of the person who, in processing information, looks down to their right (K), describes events visually, and informs you that they have trouble "getting in touch with my feelings." Now, since s/he is a walking, talking, breathing human being, the feelings and emotions must be ongoing, but for some reason the channels for bringing those feelings into conscious awareness are blocked. This can be important information for you. The person who leads with their eyes to a kinesthetic system— that is, their unconscious system is kinesthetic—but tells you things pictorially, or announce that they have trouble feeling things, or that they cannot get in touch with feelings, is someone who, in all probability, was forced to endure such physical and/or emotional pain that to protect themselves, they literally disconnected from that part of their experience. As a result, they have difficulty using their kinesthetic system as a resource. You will find that such individuals tend to have many somatic complaints.

OUT OF CONSCIOUS: RECAP

Both of the preceding examples may have been very efficacious choices at the time they were first used. For instance, if I break my leg and I have the ability to disconnect from the pain while I go to a doctor to get my leg fixed, I have used that ability to make myself more comfortable. However, if I continue to block the pain in my leg and walk around on it without getting it set, I am going to end up with gangrene and the cure will become worse than the disease.

People who appear in a therapist's office have, at some point in time, developed a cure worse than the disease. I do not want to burn my fingers, but I find that cutting my right arm off to protect my fingers is a foolish way of doing it. If I burn my fingers, they'll heal. Sewing my right arm back on may be a more difficult task. An individual who has blocked his ability to utilize one or more systems has, in effect, cut off his arm to protect his fingers. Ideally, a well-functioning human being will make use of *all* the systems, consciously and unconsciously. In addition, they will do it congruently. When their eye movements are up and they are making pictures, their description will be that of pictures; or, if their description is of feelings, they know they're making pictures and are aware of the connection between what they "see" and what they feel. When they are into their feelings, their body movements and their eye movements will be to that part of their brain that indicates they are into their kinesthetic feelings. The same would hold true for auditory.

Unfortunately, people who are not functioning well, who are in pain, tend to be making feelings out of pictures that they see in the back of their head, or they turn words into pictures into bad feelings. They do these things without awareness and, therefore, without choice. They do not deal with the world around them, but rather their inner belief system and inner reality has taken precedence over outer reality. They, in effect, use the same system to come up with the same painful memories to come up with the same painful feelings in spite of the world and the options around them. But, of course, there are those who still insist that there's no such thing as hypnosis. Yet, there are people who can sit in a perfectly quiet room with nothing going on and, in their mind, begin to hallucinate things out of the past, respond with physiological responses, and emotionally feel fear, apprehension and depression. Even if you tell them there is nothing going on around them, they continue to feel bad.

VIII
Systems — So What?

JIGSAW PUZZLES

When I was a little boy, I was given a jigsaw puzzle as a gift. When I dumped all the pieces out, I was overwhelmed. There were so many little pieces, and I did not know where to start. Someone helped me to figure out the secret. I learned to take one little piece and fit it together with another little piece until several little pieces made a bigger piece. I then learned to take a few of the bigger pieces and fit them together into still a bigger piece, until the whole puzzle was together. So, if you are feeling confused/overwhelmed at this point, I understand. I hope to help you to assemble the little pieces into bigger pieces, until you have the puzzle assembled.

What you are about to read *is not the answer,* but rather a general guide. The ways in which you can utilize systems, and the methods for doing so, are only limited by the limitations of your imagination. Once you are comfortable with the general principles, I want you to feel free to throw away the rules. As you practice, you will find what works best for you, and more importantly if you are a people-helper, what works best for your clients/patients.

It is generally agreed by therapists of all stripes that the first step to successful therapy is to establish rapport. Some schools of therapy hold that it can take up to several sessions to establish that first step. With the use of systems, I believe that rapport can, in the majority of cases, be established by learning to communicate in the individual's conscious output system (words), as well as in their unconscious system (eye movements).

SYSTEMS: GETTING STARTED

The first step for you is to listen and pay attention to the *way* the individual is expressing himself, and less to what he is saying. By paying attention to his choice of words, you will discover what his conscious output system is at that moment in time. The next step is for you to "talk in his language." It is at this stage that many therapists (and people in general) "lose" their audience. Here is an example of what *NOT* to do.

PT: Things just look hopeless. I just cannot see a way out of my problem. It is all so black and white and I feel trapped.

DR: I know how you feel. I have been stuck myself. We can make an effort to get in touch with some solid new choices that can help you to feel hope.

As you examine the above example, you may find yourself experiencing some unsettling feelings. If so, imagine what the patient might be experiencing. The patient's conscious output system was very clearly visual. As you look over his statements, I am sure you will see it. The therapist's response was very heavy into kinesthetic. As a result, the chances of establishing rapport is somewhere between slim and none. An example of what to do:

PT: Things just look hopeless. I just cannot see a way out of my problem. It is all so black and white and I feel trapped.

DR: I know that when things look dark, we can end up feeling trapped. Perhaps the two of us can find a different way of looking at this situation. When I have a more clear picture of the situation, I might be able to help you to see things you have overlooked. Remember, a box of crayons has many other colors in addition to black and white.

As you re-examine the second example, I am sure you will easily sense the difference. While our mythical doctor did not say anything concrete, his statements seemed to be right on target. I would like you to set aside some time to try "talking the other's language" to see the results for yourself. In short, listen to the conscious output system, and practice putting your responses into the individual's system. I know that if you will pay attention, you will discover how powerful a tool this is. For those of you who like excitement and adventure, practice purposefully talking in a system that is *not* your patient's conscious output system. If you watch carefully, you may see that many people will evidence pupillary dilation, altered breathing, a blank stare and a sense of not being there. We could say they may enter hypnosis. If you would like to play with that, do this: First, communicate in your patient's output system for several interchanges. Then, abruptly switch to another system, step back, shut up and observe.

PLUS (+) VERSUS MINUS (–) SYSTEM: CASE

Once you feel reasonably confident that you have identified the individual's conscious output system in the area of his/her problem, the next step is to find out if that system changes when s/he is talking about something that is pleasant. In many cases, there will be a definite switch. You can discover this by saying, for example, "When things aren't so unpleasant for you, what do you like to do?" When s/he answers, ask: "What do you like most about..." If there is a definite switch, you will have some very valuable information. You will know what systems to which to move the individual in order to help him/her feel better; what system needs cleaning up; and to start communication in the "painful" system, while slowly moving to the one s/he knows how to feel good in. The following is an example from my practice:

ME: What brings you here... That is, what would you like to have a new choice about?

PT: I've been really down. I don't have any energy, and I just don't care about anything. [This was followed by several minutes of "kinesthetic" comments.]

ME: I'm sorry you're feeling so badly. Problems can sometimes feel so heavy that we can feel good and stuck.

PT: [Nods head vigorously] Yeah. You have it. I'm just so tired of feeling this way.

ME: If I could wave a magic wand and take all those bad feelings away, what would you do that you enjoy?

PT: Paint. I love to paint. [With this statement, there was a noticeable change in her demeanor, and she appeared to be a little more relaxed.]

ME: What do you like most about painting?

PT: I like to see the painting take shape. I really enjoy putting the different colors on the canvas, and when I finish, I feel really good just looking at what I have created. [At this point, there is a definite shift to a visual output, and she is actually smiling.]

ME: What else have you seen yourself doing that you are proud of?

PT: [Pause] Oh, I know! I once designed a dress from scratch! That may not sound like much to you, but to me it was a big deal. I looked all over for a pattern that looked like what I wanted, but I couldn't find one. They either looked awful, or they wouldn't fit me. So I actually designed my own dress pattern and adjusted it to fit just me. It came out just beautiful and it looked great on me. [At this point, she is sitting up straight, with good eye contact; her voice is strong, and she looks anything but depressed.]

ME: That's great. You saw that someone else's idea of a pattern did not fit you, and you did something about it. I can see how proud of that you must be. Now I would like you to do us both a favor. I want you to close your eyes, and see yourself designing that pattern, and cutting it out. Then I want to see yourself going through all of those steps that led you to creating a pattern and dress that looked right for you. As soon as you have that picture clear in your mind, I would like you to signal *YES* by raising the first finger of your left hand. [As I said this, I reached over and lightly stroked that finger. With the emphasis on the word *yes,* and the stroking of her finger, I was setting up an ideomotor response.]

PT: OK. [Closes her eyes and continues to appear very relaxed. After a time, her finger moves up.]

ME: Thank you. Now I want you to watch that you who is so deeply involved in what she is creating...A NEW PATTERN. [This was the beginning of helping her to disassociate and to focus her on the enjoyment of creating new patterns.] I want you to pay attention to how much she is concentrating on the new pattern...the feeling of pleasure...the feeling of the scissors in her hand...the determination to design a beautiful new pattern that fits her, and helps her to really look good. [I continued to discuss her experience in great detail for close to 20 minutes. I emphasized losing track of time and place; of not paying attention to sore muscles or feelings; of solving the problem of the wrong pattern; of accepting that the patterns designed by others may not be right for her, and that she could choose to discard them and create her own.]

PT: [Opens her eyes; looks around and sighs] That was quite an experience. At first the picture was very vague, but then it became very vivid. I felt like I was floating and observing myself. After a while I could hear your voice, but it was far away, and I don't know if I paid attention. I feel very good. I know I'm looking at things in a different way, but for the life of me, I could not tell you what happened.

ME: That sounds like you had a nice learning experience, and enjoyed yourself in the process. Now our time is almost up [Pt. looks surprised, and glances quickly at her watch], but I would like to ask you something else. How would you like to attempt to paint a beautiful picture, or create a new pattern while you were blindfolded so that you had to do that by *feelings* only?

PT: [Laughs] I wouldn't. It would probably be impossible. Even if I could do it, I'm sure it would be frustrating, and I don't think I would enjoy it. I probably wouldn't like to look at the finished product.

ME: *That's Right!* I was sure you knew that, and that you only forgot for a while. Now that you see that clearly, I know you will get the picture and continue to feel better!

PT: [Looks puzzled] What? I don't know if I understand [smiles...head nods slowly yes].

ME: Good! She sees what I mean, and can show you a pleasant surprise. I will see you next week.

CASE: SECOND SESSION

PT: I really had an interesting week. For three days after I saw you, I was really floating. Things looked brighter, not only in my life, but even colors. I was much more aware of what was going on around me. On the fourth day, I crashed. I felt just as depressed as before.

ME: You don't look depressed now... In fact, you look very good.

PT: I feel great. As I was sitting around being depressed, I suddenly heard your voice. I heard you asking me how I would like to try to paint blindfolded, by feelings only. I suddenly realized that I was busy running my life by feelings without looking at other ways. Then I saw myself cutting out a dress pattern that didn't fit me, and, if I wanted it to change, I had better make a new pattern. I began to look at what I was doing to make myself so unhappy, and after a while I saw it. [She went on to explain how she would focus on everything that could go wrong; thinking "crazy" thoughts, etc.; and how she was making herself look at the whole picture, etc.] Now I would like to ask you a question.

ME: Ask away.

PT: You hypnotized me, didn't you?

ME: Well, it looked to me as if you decided to go into that state.

PT: Well, it was wonderful, only I didn't believe I could be hypnotized.

ME: It's nice to see that you are able to learn new ideas.

PT: I didn't tell you before, but I had gone to a doctor who used hypnosis, and it was a disaster. He kept telling me to feel heavy, and to sink down in the chair. The more he told me to feel heavy, the more upset I became. I thought he was telling me to be more down than I was already. So I really fought him, and never went back.

ME: Maybe he didn't know how to show you what you needed to see. [At this point, I gave her a brief lecture on the principles of the systems, and pointed out how well she responded to visual communication.]

PT: That makes sense. When I first closed my eyes, I started to get tense. Then you talked about seeing myself making the pattern, and I started to get the picture in my mind. It seemed very natural. The next thing I knew I was floating.

CASE REVIEW

Let us review the above case together. When she first explained her "problem," she was in her kinesthetic system. I began by talking to her in that system. I next asked her to recall something pleasant, and she switched into a visual output system. With that information, I was ready to help her have some new choices. I knew that I needed to help her back into her visual system, to help her have recall of more pleasant kinesthetic experiences, and to use her skills (painting and designing the dress pattern) to create a metaphor that would help her to approach her situation in a new way (pattern) and to understand just how she was creating her bad feelings. As you re-read this case, I am sure it will become very clear. Last, but not least, her comments regarding her previous experience with hypnosis should give you cause to...pause now...and recognize the importance of using the individual's system of communication.

FINE POINTS

There are a few more points about the conscious output system that I would like to have you get a handle on so that it will be very clear. A visual individual needs some time and space to "make" their pictures. If you move too close too quickly, the visual individual will usually respond with anxiety. Once a visual person has evidenced that they are comfortable with you, it is then OK to move in (slowly) and make some physical contact. On the other hand, a kinesthetic individual will feel that you are cold and unfeeling if you sit (or stand) too far away and don't make some physical contact. These two points are important. If you want to "blow" rapport in a matter of a few seconds, move in very close and touch a visual, and stand way back from a kinesthetic.

Next, where an individual is in physical pain, they are in a painful kinesthetic system. Helping them to move from kinesthetic into either visual and/or auditory will produce some profound and interesting changes. In addition, moving an individual slowly from his conscious output system to another system, and then continuing to loop through all three will, in most cases, result in the individual "taking a trip" to that "other state."

THE NEXT STEP

Once you have ascertained the individual's conscious output system in both the problem area and in a more pleasant area, you are ready for the next major step. It is now time to learn what the *unconscious* system is. Again, you will want to find out if there is a shift in the unconscious system where the individual switches from the problem to a more pleasant experience. When you have spotted the unconscious system, you are ready for some powerful work. You have what you need to begin communicating on two levels at once, and to produce so-called "informal" hypnosis without an induction or "formal" trance.

A man enters your office, sits down and begins to discuss his problem. You have discovered that his conscious output system is kinesthetic, and you are responding in kind. You next discover that his unconscious system is visual (his eyes almost always move up left and then back to you before he speaks). One choice you have is: when he finishes a statement, you look up briefly to your right (his left as he looks at you), then at him, and then "talk kinesthetically." When you finish your statement, again look up briefly to your right. In effect, you are telling him that you understand just how he is creating his experiences, and where he keeps "finding" a source for his problem. Instead of this method, or added to it, you might choose to be a mind reader. As you talk in his system (kinesthetic), you can slowly change to his unconscious system, and tell him what he is doing.

Example: "I know that you are feeling bad right now, and you're tired of those feelings, and when you become aware of those pictures from your past [move your eyes up right—his left—as he looks] and learn to stop seeing all that or to change those pictures, you will be surprised at how quickly you can feel better." With this method, many interesting things can, and often do, happen. I have had people suddenly recall past events and their attendant pain. In one instance, a man just froze, stopped breathing for several seconds, and then began to cry. He had claimed to have no feelings and to be a cold person. Most often, the individual will just stop and stare, and, in many cases, nod his or her head, or in some other way affirm what you have just said. Often, the individual will simply go into hypnosis... I forgot...there's no such thing. But, if there was, when the individual stops and stares, you may notice pupillary dilation, a marked change in breathing and other interesting "things." Sometimes, I simply say, "That's right. Now you can close your eyes and drift...and those pictures will soon be that much more clear."

MAKING UNCONSCIOUS CONSCIOUS

Another powerful approach is to simply help an individual become aware of the relationship between their unconscious system and what they are experiencing. Once they understand, it is relatively easy to help them learn to stop the process, and to change it.

Example: A 12-year-old boy, "P", with behavioral problems at school. In addition, his parents had informed me that the boy was withdrawn and nearly totally non-communicative.

ME: Well, "P" what do you think your parents brought you to see me for?

"P":   [eyes down left] I don't know. I just get into trouble a lot.

ME: Sounds to me as if you don't feel too good inside.

"P":   [eyes down left] Yeah, I feel bad.

ME: Before you started to feel bad, what did you like to do for fun?

"P":   [eyes straight ahead, then up left, then straight ahead] Baseball I guess. That's fun, and it makes me feel good.

ME: What part of baseball do you feel the best about?

"P":   [eyes up left for split second, then looks at me] I like it all, but hitting is fun. I feel good when I get a hit.

ME: I'm glad you know how to feel good [at this point I reached over and touched his arm lightly], but I think it's sad that you have been feeling so bad inside.

"P":   [eyes down left] Yeah.

ME: You must get real tired of those bad feelings, and I wonder just what that voice is telling you that makes you feel that way?

"P":   [head jerks up straight] What do you mean?

ME: I would like to help you to feel better, but I need you to help me. You don't have to tell me any secrets or anything you don't want to. [P now looks much more alert and is beginning to interact and talk with increasing ease.]

"P":   [smiles...for the first time] Sure, what do you want me to do.

ME: I want you to look up to your left and pretend that you can see yourself getting a real good hit in baseball.

"P":   OK. That's easy. [eyes up left, nods his head and grins]

ME: I can tell by your face that feels good. [He nods head yes] Now, I want you to look down to your left and find out what happens to your feelings.

"P":   [eyes down left; body slumps; facial expression changes] I feel sad again...and scared.

ME: Tell yourself *STOP!* I don't want to feel that way, and then look up to your left and see yourself hitting the ball.

"P":   [pause, head moves up, eyes up left and he smiles] Hey! That's weird. When I told myself to stop, I didn't feel scared anymore, and when I saw myself hitting the ball I started to feel good.

ME: That's great, "P." I knew you could do it. [again touched his arm] Now, I would like you to practice that all by yourself, and I'll just watch.

After several practices, "P" was having a problem keeping his eyes down to the left. Every time he began to look down to his left, his head and then his eyes would "pop" back up. He was also smiling, alert and very talkative. At this point, I knew the following: "P's" conscious output system in both his painful area and his "success" area was kinesthetic. However, there was a definite switch in his unconscious system from auditory (painful) to visual (successful). I also knew that he had some old painful tapes running in his head that were the source of his painful loop. I also knew that the next step was to help him to bring into consciousness the voice or voices he was hearing, and what was being said. That was my next task.

ME: "P," I would like you to close your eyes, and listen to the sound
        of those voices you have been hearing. You don't need to hear
        what they are saying, but just the sound, and when you hear
        that, nod your head.

"P":   [Head nods] I hear it. [sounds angry and his body tenses]

ME: Now "P," I want you to begin to see the face of the person or
        persons who match that sound, and then see the whole person,
        at about that time and place those scary things were first said.

This procedure was simply moving him from his unconscious auditory to his unconscious visual...which also resulted in "P" entering into hypnosis. Before we had finished this portion of the work he had an arm levitation as well as ideomotor responses.

ME: ["P" nods slowly] Now see that younger you at about that time
        in his life when those things happened that caused him to be sad
        and afraid. [pause...head nods yes] Now see one of your favor-
        ite baseball players taking that younger you by the hand and
        telling those people to leave you alone, and that he is going to
        protect you. Keep on watching until that younger you looks
        happy and then see him growing up strong and happy.

I saw "P" two additional times. After the first session, his parents reported that the change was like magic. He was talkative, helping around the house, and getting along in school. And he had told his parents that he didn't like it when they yelled at each other, and that when they did he was going to go somewhere and not worry. Two years later I saw his mother for another matter, and she reported that his "problems" never came back. (By the way, I have "blown" them just as dramatically as I have been successful.)

SYSTEM INTERRUPTIONS

Another very powerful method of restructuring an individual's unconscious pattern is to interpret the painful pattern, and direct the individual to their successful one. For example, the individual looks up left for a split second, and then looks straight ahead when s/he is discussing some positive experience. When s/he begins to talk about the area of difficulty, the eyes go up left, then down left (auditory) then down right while s/he discusses a painful situation. The next time s/he begins to talk about the problem, you snap your fingers at the moment s/he starts to move his/her eyes down left. In addition, you ask them, or signal them, to look at you while they talk. The result will be: that you have directed them into using the unconscious successful pattern—in this case, eyes up left, then straight ahead.

A variation of this method would be to help the individual overlay the successful unconscious pattern onto the problem area. For example, a 10-year-old boy who had developed an almost phobic response to his father's (angry) voice. In his areas of success, he was visual both in his conscious and unconscious system. He was asked to "listen" to the sound of his father's voice in his mind. Then I helped him to change the picture of his father into increasingly humorous ones. The last picture was of his father standing and yelling while in a pair of old underwear that was full of holes. In less than 20 minutes, his "phobic" response was broken up. He was told to keep his new picture a secret, which he did. It has been over a year, and he has never had a reoccurrence of his problem. (I also had a brief session with the father and helped him to realize the effect his yelling was producing. His wife later reported that he had substantially reduced his yelling, but that when he did, her son seemed unaffected.)

MASTERING OUT OF CONSCIOUS

The next area for you to begin mastering is that of the out of conscious unconscious system (out of conscious system). That is of particular importance in the area of the individual's dysfunction. For example, a patient's conscious output system is kinesthetic, while the input system is visual, and you do not observe any evidence of his/her using the auditory system to check out "reality." The indication here is that the auditory is the out of conscious system. Another example, using the same systems as above: you ask the individual what s/he is seeing in his/her mind and the reply is, "I'm not seeing any pictures"—or words to that effect—equals out of conscious visual. Another pattern might be: Patient looks up left, then down left and the conscious output system is very visual. This could indicate that the kinesthetic is the out of conscious system; or, if you were to ask what s/he is saying to him/herself and the response is, "I'm not saying anything" or "I don't hear anything" equals out of conscious auditory.

OUT OF CONSCIOUS TO CONSCIOUS

Once you have determined which is the out of conscious system, you have two primary choices: to bring that system into conscious awareness so that the individual stops giving him/herself hypnotic suggestions for which there is then "amnesia," or to use that system as the one in which you structure your hypnotic and therapeutic work. Since that system is out of conscious, almost any hypnotic work you do in that system will, in most cases, lead to amnesia for that work. When that happens, it makes it very difficult for your patient to "block" or "sabotage" the therapeutic process.

If you choose the first method—bringing the system into awareness—you have several choices. The easiest, and in most cases the fastest, is to do system overlays. That simply means starting in the individual's conscious system, moving to the unconscious system and then to the out of conscious system, and repeating the procedure until you get the desired results.

Let us say that the patient's auditory is the out of conscious system, while visual is the conscious output, and, to make it easy, kinesthetic is the unconscious system. (By the way, what I have just described is an unusual combination. I picked it to make my job of clarification easier for me.) Let us also say that your patient has informed you that s/he really likes to go to the beach. You might then ask him/her to close his/her eyes and picture the beach on a beautiful day. As your patient responds, you would then spend a few minutes describing visual experiences common to the beach. As you observe signs of relaxation, or calmness, or concentration, or even trance, you would then begin to introduce kinesthetic experiences: e.g., watching the beautiful blue sky and the clouds, and feeling the warmth from that bright sun. After a few minutes of visual/kinesthetic, you would begin to introduce the auditory experience: "And the sound of the waves crashing in helps you to relax even more, and as you hear the sounds of the waves, you watch the waves building and then falling, you feel a deep calmness. You can see children playing and hear the sound of their laughter, and remember a feeling of pleasure from your past," etc., etc.

With system overlaying, one of two things will happen; in many cases, *both* will happen. Your patient will move into that state of mind that we might call hypnosis, and, perhaps more slowly and with more "experiences" of system overlay, the out of conscious system's "block" will crumble. I have had dozens of individuals report that, as they experienced what I was describing, they began to hear the sounds clearly, or feel all the feelings, or get clear pictures. What is even more important is that in subsequent sessions they report and give evidence of "cleaning up" that block in their real world. Try it...you'll like it.

UNBLOCKING VIA COMMON EXPERIENCE

Another approach to the unblocking of an out of conscious system is to begin simply talking about common, pleasant experiences in that system: e.g., out of conscious kinesthetic = talk about what it feels like to take a warm shower after a hard day's work; the feelings of a freshly laundered sheet when you get into bed; the warm afterglow of making love. Use your imagination, almost anything will do it. If, as you are describing common feelings, you begin to more and more describe pleasant feelings of childhood, you will stand a good chance of producing hypnosis and a regression to their childhood. This will happen because your communication will cause them to have to go into their out of conscious system in order to find that experience. Once the individual goes into that system, they must leave their conscious output system somewhere else. In short, an altered state of consciousness.

UTILIZING OUT OF CONSCIOUS SYSTEM

If you make the choice of leaving the out of conscious system just that—out of conscious—your approach would be very different from what you have read thus far. You could use that system to "mind read" and provoke internal searches. Let us assume that the individual has an out of conscious auditory system. You could say something like: "And soon you will remember just who that person was that said those things that are still causing you to feel that way," or: "And I know that as you become aware of what that voice is saying, you will know how to solve that problem." Such an approach will "stir up" a lot of internal activity, and generally will cause the individual to soon discover what that auditory system is doing.

Another use of the out of conscious system is to use it to produce amnesia for beneficial suggestions. Example: A patient whose conscious output system was visual, while her out of conscious system was kinesthetic. She told me that "everything looks hopeless. When I see the way people look at me I really get upset." I asked her to tell me what the sound of hopelessness was. Her face went blank; she looked confused, and, after a moment, her eyes went down left, then up left. At that point,

I said, "OK, instead you can begin to feel stronger and feel more calm."
She looked at me and said, "What? I didn't hear what you said." Since
my "suggestion" was made in her out of conscious system, while she was
using her other systems to search, she had amnesia for my words. As this
session progressed, she became very relaxed. As we finished she said,
"I'm not sure what happened today, but I feel much more calm, and I
think I may be strong enough to beat this."

THE SHOCK METHOD

There is one more approach to the out of conscious system I would
like to give you: The shock method. With this approach, you simply
ignore the conscious and unconscious system, and go straight to the out
of conscious system. Example: Conscious output system equals kinesthetic; unconscious input system equals auditory; out of conscious system equals visual. The patient is talking "kinesthetically" about how bad
s/he feels. You respond, "When you see what those feelings look like, I
know you will be able to change the picture to one that looks much
better." With this method, you have a good chance of producing amnesia
for what you have said, causing an informal hypnotic state for a moment
(or much longer) and/or producing an unconscious restructure without
the patient being aware of how all of this took place.

CASE 5: "R"

I would now like to tell you about "R" and how the use of systems
made the difference between success and a great big zero. "R" was
brought to my office by his wife, and as I soon learned, he had not really
agreed to see me. He refused to fill out my intake form, and when he
came into my office he would not talk. He sat with his arms tightly
crossed and gave every evidence of being very hostile. His wife informed
me that "R" had not been his usual self for nearly a year; that she had
taken him to a psychiatrist and he had refused to cooperate; and that he
would not tell her what was bothering him. I asked him what he thought
the trouble was, and his response was to merely shrug his shoulders. The
only other information I had was that "R" stared to his left, with his eyes
in a slightly upward mode. Since he wouldn't talk, I began to use
metaphors with my emphasis on visual experiences. I talked about a little
boy being afraid and angry. Each story was filled with visual information. After about 10 minutes, "R" began glancing at me, and would
occasionally nod his head. As he appeared to be starting to respond (very

slightly at this point), I began to tie in kinesthetic experiences to my stories; e.g., "...and the little boy couldn't see any way out of his problem, which caused him to feel a very heavy feeling inside." "R" now began to stare freely at me and his body posture relaxed slightly. However, even though he was now looking in my direction, it was clear to me that he was now in an altered state. His eyes had a far-away distracted look, and his facial muscles had flattened out. Several minutes later he looked right at me, blinked several times, and interrupted me to say, "I get the picture. If I don't look for a way out of this, I'll never see things differently." He then began to talk quite freely. He said that he had been very depressed about his children leaving home, and by the "fact" that he was getting on in years (he was 62) without ever having seen himself successful. He also admitted that not only hadn't he wanted to see me, but that he had come in prepared to be very hostile. (I discovered later that he believed that seeking help was a sign of his failure, and he didn't want to "face" that.)

CASE 6: CHANGE

At this juncture, "R" was actually very friendly and talkative. His "problem" just poured out, almost always beginning with his visual system and ending in his kinesthetic. Since he was using a ton of words, I made the following assumptions as to his systems: His output system was primarily auditory, with visual being a strong second. His unconscious system was visual (very pronounced) and since he never moved his eyes to the kinesthetic or auditory, my best guess was that both his kinesthetic and auditory were out of conscious. He verified my assumptions when he told me, "I have a lot of trouble feeling close to people or showing any emotions, and my wife tells me that I don't listen to people very well."

I spent several minutes discussing the processes of unconscious learning, emphasizing visual experiences. I then said, "I would like you to see for yourself how the unconscious can work separately from the conscious. I want you to hold your hand in front of your face like this." At this point I "show" him with my hand, palm toward my face.

"Good. Now, as you watch your hand just like that, your unconscious will show you something you need to see... Perhaps that little boy at a time and place where he began to see himself as not good enough. [Pause] That's right...and as that picture becomes more clear, that hand will begin to bring that picture closer toward your face, while the sound of my voice makes you feel stronger." His hand begins slowly moving toward his face.

"Now, as you get the picture [using the exact phrase he had used earlier], you may find the comfort of closing your eyes [blinks several times and then his eyes close], and I really don't know just where you will see that hand coming to rest against your face, as my voice relaxes you more and more. I know it will be strange to see that picture of the little boy who feels bad while you feel comfortable even more...now."

His hand reaches his face after several minutes, and he appears to be very deep into "that state." "Now, as you continue to learn something important to you, you can continue to change the feelings into those of comfort, and I don't want that hand to move down any more quickly than...*YOU HAVE LEARNED SOMETHING IMPORTANT,* and that is no more quickly than you hear the voice inside telling the little boy that it will be OK, and that it never was what he thought it was."

It was close to ten minutes before "R's" hand began moving down, and when it was on his lap, he opened his eyes. He began to cry softly (pretty good for a man who has trouble feeling or showing his feelings), and told me about two incidents that had really "got to him" as a child. His eyes were now moving to the kinesthetic area when he was recalling the feelings of those incidents, and several times they went briefly to his auditory. He informed me that sometimes he heard my voice, but most of the time he didn't, and that he could remember very little about what I had said.

The example of "R" is but a small example of what systems can do for you, and, more importantly, for your patients/clients. I know that this "trip" through the land of systems has led you to "see" many new sights, as well as touch upon many interesting points, and I hope that the sounds were stimulating also. Even though this trip is ending, you have only started. As you practice, you will discover that I have only touched lightly on all the possibilities that you will soon see.

It is far beyond the scope of this work to get into all of the ramifications, subtleties and surprises. One of the surprises I hope that you will soon discover is this: All systems, from anxiety to depression, anorexia to obesity, will have certain set patterns or systems. I will go more out on a limb and state that the majority of people with each symptom will have the same patterns. Once you recognize the pattern and its loop, you need to help the individual break it, and form a choice of patterns.

Now that you have shed some, and maybe all, of the excess baggage you began with, your hands are free to get a firm grasp on new things, and I hope you will find the rest of this book a journey forward with comfort...NOW.

IX

Patterns

HYPNOSIS AND PATTERNS

Picture, if you will, an old time hypnotist putting a subject into a hypnotic state and then giving a powerful suggestion. (For those of you who are wondering just what a powerful suggestion is: Those that work are powerful; the rest are weak.) The hypnotist suggests that at 4:00 in the afternoon, the subject's nose will itch and the subject will have to scratch it. If this suggestion were effective, the subject would respond as expected. If he were to repeat this response three or four days in a row, he might be surprised to discover that he had developed a pattern of scratching his nose at 4:00 P.M. each day. Even an individual without training in hypnosis would recognize that the pattern was the result of the hypnotic suggestion. Of course!

Take a child and tell him, over and over, that he will never be as good as his father, nor as his brother, and that he will never amount to anything. Years later, every time he is about to get a promotion, he gets drunk and "forgets" to show up for work, and he amounts to nothing. We wouldn't call that a pattern resulting from hypnosis...or would we?

Patterns are a necessary and important part of our behavior. Most patterns serve as useful functions, and free our mind for new learning experiences. In reading this you are relying on patterns learned many years ago: patterns in sitting, holding the book, seeing the words, understanding, and learning.

You drive down a street and a car runs a red light right in front of you. Automatically, you jam on the brakes, tighten up and prepare for the possibility of a crash. During those actions, there were literally hundreds of physiological, psychological and emotional responses occurring in a patterned way, designed to help you. If you had to "think" out and analyze the situations and your responses, you no doubt would have had an accident.

PATTERNS: AN EXPERIMENT

We humans not only rely on patterns, but, as I will point out shortly, we are capable of adopting patterns in a very rapid fashion. In addition, we are uncomfortable—sometimes even miserable—when our patterns are interfered with or changed. Think back...now...to a time when you moved, changed jobs or even rearranged your furniture. You may be able to remember those vague uneasy feelings. You may even experience some of that now or in a short while.

Try the following experiment: Pay attention to your sequence (pattern) of dressing in the morning. Do you put your pants on before your shirt? Right shoe before the left? Blouse before your skirt? Shave the right side of your face before the left? Cheeks before the neck? Once you have discovered your patterns, make every effort to vary your patterns each day for several days. You may notice that you feel awkward and a little clumsy. Next, change the side of the bed you normally sleep on. Be prepared! You may have some difficulty falling asleep. On the other hand, you may not sleep well at all. If you sleep with someone, and I hope you do, and if they agree to change sides with you, share your experience the next morning. Last, but not least, if you eat a meal in a family setting, have everyone take a different seat from the patterned ones you usually take. Pay close attention to your internal responses, and observe the behavior of those around you.

It has been estimated that at least 60% to 70% of all our behaviors are patterned responses. Patterns can free us for more creative endeavors. Maladaptive and self-defeating behaviors are patterned responses also. In my opinion, therapy succeeds, by whatever method or construction, whenever painful patterns are interrupted and more successful patterns are utilized in their place.

There are biological patterns built into the system, but the ones we wish to explore are learned. What can be learned can be relearned. We all know how to crawl and we always will. However, we have also learned how to walk, and find that to be, in most cases, a better choice. We know when crawling would be our most effective choice and can decide when to rely on that pattern. People who rely on maladaptive patterns often appear to have no choice as to when or where to use another pattern. A maladaptive behavior may be totally inappropriate under the circumstances, or it may have served a purpose in the past and now be archaic. Or, the painful results may be due to a lack of choices as to when to rely on the pattern.

PAIN AS A PATTERN

Physiological pain is more than pain. It, too, is a pattern. The individual suffering pain from illness or injury responds to that pain in a patterned way. The pattern is based on their past experience with pain, their belief system as to their ability to deal with pain, as well as their future expectations. The individual whose past experience and belief system lead them to expect that they can handle it—that they've always done OK, and they "know" that they will recover quickly—becomes what is called a "reducer." As the name implies, these individuals are able not only to minimize their response to pain, they are also able to actually lower their perception of the pain itself. At the other end of the scale is what is called an "augmenter." An augmenter's belief system, and therefore their remembered history of pain, is that pain is terrible, awful, always gets worse, and they can't stand it. Their future expectation is that the pain will always get worse before it gets better.

This patterned response of thinking leads to the patient who interprets twinges, the itching of healing, pressure, gas after surgery, etc., as signals of pain, and, as if by black magic or negative hypnosis, they actually experience more pain. Augmenters recover from illness or surgery more slowly, with more complications, and more complaints than a reducer. To reason with an augmenter, or argue, or give up and walk away in disgust, is to forget that their belief system and pattern of response is, in effect, operating as a hypnotic suggestion. Logic and reason have little or less to do with it. So keep on forgetting…forgetting to use logic.

Just as a pattern can be an effective and automatic response producing beneficial results, so too can a pattern be an effective and automatic method for self-defeat. If an individual combines a belief system such as, "I can't succeed, I always fail," with a pattern of behavior that leads to self-defeat, he not only fails, but the failure itself "proves" his belief system. This leads to reinforcement of the automatic patterns of belief and behavior. It is well-known in scientific and academic communities that an individual can state a hypothesis, and then find the data and statistics to prove the theory. This principle also holds true for belief systems and patterns. A belief system leads to automating a response that leads to proving the belief system that leads to repetition of the pattern. It is almost like the proverbial snake eating its own tail and complaining about its imminent demise.

G.A. Miller, E. Galanter and K.H. Pribram *(Plans and the Structure of Behavior,* 1960) point out that habits and skills are plans that begin as voluntary processes, but in the process of repeating and overlearning become fixed and automatic.

HYPNOSIS — PATTERNS — ERICKSON

In the section on therapeutic applications, we will discuss, in more detail, methods for interrupting self-defeating patterns of behavior, and we will help you to develop patterns for understanding and discovering patterns. For now, consider the results of sudden pattern interruption.

Several years ago, researchers decided to interrupt hypnotic subjects as they were performing post-hypnotic tasks. They found something quite interesting. The subject, upon being interrupted, spontaneously entered into a hypnotic state. Milton Erickson utilized this phenomenon as a method of trance induction. For example, he would give a suggestion for some post-hypnotic activity to take place at the next session. Dr. Erickson would then interrupt the pattern. The subject not only entered into the hypnotic state, in many cases the subject developed spontaneous amnesia for the events just preceding the trance state. If you, as a therapist, can discover a pattern in your patient, and lead the patient to recreate it, and interrupt it before completion, you may be surprised. You might find the individual entering into the hypnotic state. I may be wrong. You may not be surprised at all.

CASE 7: PATTERN INTERRUPTION

A woman entered my office, sat down, tightly crossed her legs, then crossed her arms over her chest, let out a deep sigh and began spewing out words. The words were about her hopeless situation, her stupidity, her inability to do anything right, and that she probably couldn't even learn "this hypnotic stuff." At that point, my phone rang. Since I was expecting an important call, I had not turned it off. The woman looked upset, so I apologized and had her wait in the reception room while I completed the call. When I asked her back in, she sat in the same chair, and recreated her initial behavior in every detail: tightly crossed her legs, then her arms, deep sigh, and then the stream of words of helplessness.

Recognizing her behavior as a probable pattern, I decided to interrupt it. I said sharply, "Wait, I can't hear you from there. Would you mind moving to that other chair so I can hear you better?" She moved to the other chair, crossed her legs, then arms, then sighed, but before she could spew, I turned to my desk and began writing without a glance at her. Next, I apologized and told her that the first chair would be better and she could help me by moving back. As she sat down, I told her to please cross her legs and only then her arms. As she complied, she developed what Dr. Erickson calls "responsive attentiveness" (Erickson, Rossi 1976). The best description of this might be "staring in an almost day-dreaming way."

She was then told to close her eyes and take a deep breath and let it out slowly (i.e., her sigh described differently) before we could talk. As she complied (already responding to my lead and suggestions), she was then told, "Now that you are becoming so much more relaxed, you can continue breathing slowly, relaxing that much more [leaving it to her to figure out how much is that much more], and soon you may want to uncross just your arms or just your legs first [implying there would be a second uncrossing without knowing when]." Within two minutes, a most satisfactory state had been achieved.

As you analyze the preceding example, you may grasp now the importance of the recognition and interruption and potential of patterns. It was a better than even bet that the woman's behavior was a patterned response in approaching any problem. Since she was in my office asking for help, it was also a good bet that her pattern was not working. Her pattern was first interrupted before she could get into her words of despair (sent her to another chair). She was then interrupted again, this time before her sigh (sent her back to the first chair). Her pattern was again interrupted and *directed* (cross your legs and only then your arms) and further interrupted by the injection of "close your eyes and take a deep breath and let it out slowly before we can talk." In summary, her pattern was interrupted, then redirected and then redirected again into a formal hypnotic state.

INSTANT PATTERN

Patterns, whether graceful and efficacious or painful and destructive, can be established rather rapidly. In his work on split brain, Gazzaneza (1967) discussed what he termed "conditional reflex, or bad habit" and the rapidity with which an individual can learn such patterns of behavior when he said:

We must remember that we are examining a half of the human
brain, a system easily capable of learning from a single trial in a test.
— *The Split Brain in Man* by Michael S. Gazzanega,
August 1967, p. 372 "Progress in Psychobiology"
Readings from *Scientific American,* W.F. Freeman & Co.

At our training seminars, I will have a volunteer hold out either their
right or left arm straight ahead, making a fist with their arm very, very
stiff. I then tell them I am going to give them an instruction that is
impossible to carry out: I'm going to ask them to raise their arm up and
move it down at the same time. Of course, it's impossible to go in two
directions at the same time. I then state, "Begin." While they stare at me
in disbelief, I say, "That's right, now you can *BLINK.*" I emphasize
"blink" with my voice. At that moment in time, the person will blink.
You could imagine that the brain is saying, "What is this craziness? I
can't raise my arm up and move it down at the same time." But when
they hear, "You can blink," the brain says, "Of course, I can do that."
Now, the interesting thing is how quickly that suggestion is accepted.
What is even more interesting is, if you ask that person within a minute
or two after their first trial to raise that arm and hold it up again, in most
cases, s/he will automatically blink as s/he brings the arm up. In effect,
the beginning of a pattern has been established in seconds. If s/he were to
repeat this raising of the arm and blinking for four, five or ten times in a
day, s/he might develop what is called a conditioned reflex, or a bad
habit.

If, as I believe, a conditioned response can be produced that quickly,
imagine what happens when a person is raised hearing certain statements
about limitations, or having certain kinds of painful incidents happening
over and over. If, in a matter of seconds, we can learn to put out our right
arm and blink at the same time, what would happen to a child or an adult
hearing something said over and over when it's connected with a
demonstration of how they are supposed to behave.

For example, consider the woman who sees her mother drunk all the
time and whose father says, "You're just like your mother, don't be that
way." The child grows up and behaves just like her mother while
protesting that she doesn't want to be that way, carrying out both ends of
the suggestion.

The combination of internal belief systems (brought about by traumas, suggestions, or what have you), and the repetition of patterns of
behavior that reinforce belief systems, simply results in an individual

who is stuck and without choice. You must look not at what the world is doing to them, but rather what they are doing within the world based on what belief system and what patterns. Since a form of hypnosis has been used to convince them that things exist which do not exist, or that things do not exist which do exist, it would seem to me that a hair of the dog might be the best course of action. In short, if a person really believed they could be successful, they wouldn't need you to tell them, "Of course you can be successful." It seems ridiculous that somebody becomes, let us say, a psychiatrist or a psychologist with years and years of schooling, and spends time telling a patient something obvious such as, "Of course you can be successful. There are opportunities in this world." So, the real problem is how to interrupt the pattern of behavior that continues to reinforce the belief system, and how to help the patient examine their own belief system, to help them acknowledge other choices that are available in the world.

While we will specifically with the application of these principles later in this book, a selected case will help you to tie together what you have learned thus far. If you find yourself still tied to the past, this case will help you cut that cord right at the Knot yesterday but now!

PATTERNS: BELIEF SYSTEMS — CASE STUDY

I was asked to see a man who was suffering with intractable pain resulting from cancer that had metastasized throughout his skeletal system. Other than his name, age and diagnosis, the only other information I had was: the pain had become so severe that he was talking about suicide; medication was becoming less and less effective; he was willing to see a hypnotist, but he doubted that hypnosis or anything would help. Based on this information, I reasoned that asking him to relax in order to become hypnotized, or to attempt to teach him to control his pain at the start, or to explain theory to him, would be the height of illogical therapy. I agreed to see the man providing that everyone concerned—except the patient—would be aware of and accept that I would use unexpected and unorthodox methods.

When I arrived at his home, I was taken immediately to his den where I found him standing up, hunched over and evidencing great pain. His face was contorted, his body twisted and emaciated. As I walked toward him, his physician said, "This is Doctor Heller, the hypnotist I told you about." With a feeble and apparently painful movement, he put his hand out to shake mine. I pushed his hand to the side with the heel of my right hand and I hit him on the forehead with enough force to jar him. He stared at me with shock and disbelief on his face and said, "What did you do that for?" Using a harsh tone of voice I said, "Shut up unless I ask you." (Leaving what I might ask unspoken). At this point, he was standing up almost straight and his look of disbelief and shock was even more apparent. I went on in the same tone and said, "I am now going to stomp on the top of your foot and break all the little bones." He said in a pleading voice, "Please don't hurt me." I replied harshly, "I have to hurt you," and with that, I raised my right foot over his left. His voice which was no longer weak said, "Don't." I replied even more harshly, "Shut your eyes, take a deep breath and relax… I can't hurt a man when his eyes are closed." He closed his eyes in one split second, took a deep breath and slowly exhaled. As he exhaled, I began to talk softly, his face relaxed, then his body, and, within a moment, he was not only comfortable (he had escaped me), but somehow he had entered into a profound hypnotic state.

CASE EXPLANATION

You might be wondering about the crazy behavior just described. Good question; I'm glad you asked. Since the man's present problem was intractable pain, I could assume that, at least in his present situation, he was in his kinesthetic system. As stated earlier, you must go where your patient is: that is, meet them in their world. Therefore, I knew I would not only need to begin in some kinesthetic way, but in a manner that would supersede his kinesthetic reality. I also knew that his belief system included: he had pain; it was getting worse; nothing was going to help; everyone was trying to make me feel better, but to no avail. I could further assume that he had patterned expectations about doctors, what they do and how they act, as well as to his pain itself.

The pain pattern would include putting all or most of his attention on the pain, expecting it to get worse, becoming more anxious and depressed, feeling hopeless and thereby increasing his pain perception. My behavior interrupted his patterns; his attention went from his pain to my crazy behavior; he stopped worrying about what he felt and began worrying about what I would do and what he would feel as a result. My behavior was a "shade" different from what he expected based on his belief about doctors; everyone was trying to help him feel less pain, while I seemed to be hell-bent on causing him more. Since the human organism is designed to protect itself, the moment he was given the option to protect himself (shut your eyes, take a deep breath, etc.) he took it. As soon as he closed his eyes, several of his past beliefs had changed or were changing. By closing his eyes, he could stop something from happening instead of believing he couldn't do anything to help himself; his belief system about his pain began to change.

Once he closed his eyes and began to relax, his level of pain lowered—something he hadn't believed possible. He learned he could avoid more pain, which also taught him he could *have* less and he could control something to do with pain. Most of his new discoveries were inferential: "shut your eyes, etc.," equaled you can do something to avoid more pain (my stomping on him). If you can feel less and avoid pain, you can control pain. Last, but not least, when I said, "Shut up unless I ask," the response was not connected to what he had asked. The words "shut up" and "unless I ask" implied he was to shut up and I would ask something of him. As a result of this "subtle" approach, the patient not only became comfortable and discovered hope, he was also able to learn self-hypnosis, to change his kinesthetic pain to visual pictures, and to disassociate from his body.

PATTERNS: PRACTICE

Now, I am going to ask those of you who are people-helpers to interrupt your patterns, as well as the patterns of your clients/patients. These exercises should help you expand your belief systems or merely change them.

Pay attention to the body positions your clients/patients assume when they are discussing problems, and compare that with their positions when they are discussing something pleasant. Next, when they get into problem areas, politely interrupt them, and help them to assume the position they use when talking about pleasant things. They, and you, may find that they have trouble getting back to the problem. Ask a few patients to talk about their problems in one specific chair and to move from that chair for all other conversations. Observe the changes as they move from one chair to another. Next, when they discuss a problem, interrupt and have them describe a pleasant vacation or something they do well. Ask another patient to laugh and smile as he discusses a problem and observe what happens.

As for the therapist, switch chairs with your patient; look away from a patient during problem talk and make eye contact during pleasant conversations; cough repeatedly during problem talk; smile during pleasant talk and nod your head. You may discover that your patient begins to understand, on an unconscious level, that feeling good, and thinking pleasant thoughts, gets your attention. Use non-sequiturs:

PT: Doctor, I've been very depressed.

DR: Speaking of baseball, who do you think will win the world series? And, while you are doing that, take several deep breaths before you close your eyes.

PT: I've been very depressed.

DR: Splendid! I'm glad you're getting it out of the way. By the way, where did you go for your high school graduation?

Begin to observe your way of relating to patients. How do you greet people? Vary it. What facial expressions do you rely on? Mix them up and practice new ones. Learn to use certain tonal and speed patterns when discussing pleasant topics. Then, when your patient is in a bad place, use your pleasant tonal pattern. Without your patient's conscious awareness, you interrupt their pain-producing pattern and they will usually cheer right up. Remember, there's no such thing as hypnosis without trance, or patterns without blueprints...or maybe there is.

X

Left Meets Right Meets Left

TWO BRAINS

If asked, most people would insist that they are rational and that they would respond to reality. I would ask of them: "Which reality?" Within each of us there reside (at least) two separate, distinct, different and equal realities. One "reality" is that of the left hemisphere of the brain (LH) and the other is that of the right hemisphere (RH).

Professor Betty Edwards (1978) conveys the general consensus of brain researches when she states that not only do the two hemispheres specialize, they also perceive reality in their own unique way. The left hemisphere specializes in verbal skills, numbers, analytical thinking and linear, digital reasoning. The right hemisphere specializes in spatiality, visual imagery, imagination, color, rhythm, kinesthetic experience, and creativity (Ornstein, 1973; Edwards, 1978; Buzan and Dixon, 1978). As Robert Ornstein (1972) puts it:

> Both the structure and function of these two "half brains" in some part underline the two modes of consciousness which simultaneously coexist within each one of us. Although each hemisphere shares the potential for many functions, and both sides participate in most activities, in the normal person the two hemispheres tend to specialize.

When you see someone you already know, your left hemisphere recognizes each specific feature: i.e., the nose, mouth, eyes, etc. However, if only your left hemisphere were operating, you would not be able to recognize the whole. Your right hemisphere, with its spatial and conceptual ability, takes the specific pieces and makes a whole. Dr. Roger Sperry of the California Institute of Technology, along with his associates Joseph

Bogen, Michael Gazzaneza, et al., have demonstrated this concept in their research with split brain patients (epileptics in which the corpus callosum—the arched bridge of nervous tissue that connects the two cerebral hemispheres and allows communication between the right and left sides of the brain—has been surgically cut).

SPERRY: SPLIT BRAIN RESEARCH

In one of the now classical experiments by the Sperry group, split brain patients were given the task of assembling a jigsaw puzzle while they were in a situation that allowed only left-hemisphere function. Films of these experiments show the patient struggling with the pieces and then failing to put the pieces where they belong. One film shows an even more provocative phenomenon: One subject was busy trying to find where the pieces went using his right hand (left hemisphere) and suddenly, without his left-hemisphere awareness, he received help. The film shows his left hand (right hemisphere) sneaking into the picture and correcting the right hand until the experimenter forces the intruder away.

HEMISPHERIC CYCLES

Psychologists at Dalhousie University have been investigating what is termed the 90-minute cycle of the brain. During their research, they have been able to verify a specific hemispheric pattern: When left-hemisphere activities are at their peak, right-hemisphere activities are at their lowest ebb. Conversely, when right-hemispheric activities are at their peak, left-hemisphere activity is at its lowest ebb.

Since different tasks require different hemispheric activity, we might wonder what would happen if one were to over rely on one hemisphere and under utilize the other; or rely on the wrong hemisphere for the task at hand. (As you continue to wonder, the possible answers will become clear.) In their book, *The Evolving Brain,* Buzan and Dixon (cited) demonstrate an historical trend in which western societies have continued to place a greater emphasis on left-hemisphere functions while tending to ignore and denigrate right-hemisphere aspects: "Western society has placed a greater emphasis on the scientific and analytical side of mental functioning than it has on the more colorful and imaginistic side."

They also build a strong case for "united we stand, divided we fall" as to the relationship of hemispheric functions. Since different tasks and activities require different mental skills, it would stand to reason that both hemispheres are required if we are to move toward our unique potentials. Conversely, I believe there is a direct correlation between over reliance on left hemisphere and instability, suicide and craziness. It is almost as if the right hemisphere, finding itself imprisoned, attempts to break out of "jail" in any way it knows how.

> [The brain] can love and hate together, it can be calculating and irrational at the same time, it can value trees and enjoy the endless newsprint which is destroying them. It has a left and right hemisphere which only appears to oppose when one is used at the "expense of the other."   — Buzan and Dixon 1978, p. 129

To reverse the trend toward over utilization of one hemisphere at "the expense of the other," I believe left must meet right must meet left.

In discussing split brain patients, Ornstein (1972, p. 76) drew a parallel between the results of a surgical disconnection of hemispheres, and the results of a so-called emotional disconnect when he stated:

> In this instance, a clear split was observed between the two independent consciousnesses that are normally in communication and collaboration. In such experiments with split brain patients, we can accurately localize the split of information in the system. A similar process, although much more difficult to localize, may underlie the classic Freudian symptoms of repression and denial, both situations in which the verbal mechanism has no access to emotional information in other parts of the system. In less pathological instances, when we perform an action "intuitively," our words often make no sense, perhaps because the action has been initiated by a part of the brain little involved in language.

HEMISPHERIC: OVERVIEW

While brain hemispheric research has demonstrated that both hemispheres have the raw potential of the other, in practicality, the right hemisphere has very little in the way of developed verbal skill. Where certain stroke victims have been helped to speak again, through right-hemispheric training, they begin speaking at about the level of a five-year-old child. Therefore, while it is probably safe to assume that the left hemisphere speaks for us, it is not safe to assume that the right hemisphere does not communicate.

On the contrary, the right hemisphere communicates in many ways, some delightful and graceful, and others painful: dreams, fantasies, hunches, "gut feelings" and kinesthetic memories, to name but a few. All of the communication methods of the right hemisphere are important, but, for the purposes of this work, we will focus on two forms of right-hemispheric communications.

First, there is mounting evidence that the right hemisphere, with its built-in ability to effect and mediate autonomic nervous system processes, is responsible for the formation of so-called psychosomatic or psychogenic symptomology (Furia, 1973; Galin, 1974; Erickson and Rossi, 1979) and that these symptoms are a metaphoric communication of the right hemisphere (Erickson, Rossi & Rossi, 1979; Heller *Meta 4 Change,* in work).

Secondly, in my opinion, we do not develop any behavior, no matter how bizarre, unless at some point in our history we come to "believe," at some level, that the behavior was necessary to protect ourselves in the best way we knew at the time. Therefore, so-called irrational fears, anxieties and depressions are messages from our right-hemispheric memory bank that we are entering into "real or imagined" danger zones.

If, as many brain researchers contend, western cultures are beginning to rely on over utilization of the left hemisphere, what are the possible consequences to the individual? Empirical observation and review might be a very rewarding learning experience as well as the beginning of an answer. I would ask you to observe the people around you with special emphasis in the therapeutic situation. I believe you will discover that those individuals who would fit into the so-called "rigid compulsive" and/or "perfectionist" category: will evidence over utilization of left-hemispheric skills; are logical to the extreme (once you believe a turtle is a horse you may very logically attempt to saddle and ride it); are analytical about nearly everything (try making love analytically by the numbers); lack general spontaneity; tend to seriousness often without a well-developed sense of humor; tend to plan all activities in minute detail.

These left-hemispheric individuals will often be your typical ulcer, heart attack or alcoholic patient, as if their right hemisphere was trying to escape. On the other hand, you will discover that those individuals who fit under the categories of "impulsive," "hysterical," "hysterical conversion," "acting out behavior" and even "crazy" are evidencing almost total right-hemispheric activity. It is as if they have given up trying to live within the narrow confines of left hemisphere, and have escaped into the fantasy world of right hemisphere. (Some researchers have postulated that schizophrenia is merely the dream process acted out in "reality.")

I'm not suggesting that all people will fit neatly into the above right hemisphere/left hemisphere categories. However, many will come close enough to give you pause for thought.

> The way an individual deals with a situation either analytically, holistically or a mixture of the two, apparently reflects the brain's style. Reliance on "left brain" strategies in all situations would characterize an extremely analytical person. A right-brained person, in contrast, appears more emotional and rarely analyzes.
> — *Brain Mind Bulletin,* January 7, 1980, Vol. 5, No. 4

HEMISPHERIC: BELIEF SYSTEMS

Another major consideration as to a dichotomy between right hemisphere and left hemisphere concerns belief systems. The individual locked into left hemisphere will tend to take the same facts and apply the same logical sequences to arrive at the same painful solution and, from that, logically conclude their belief is accurate. After all, if a computer is misprogrammed, it will rapidly and perfectly arrive at the wrong answer.

A "mythical" example might make the point more clear. Quite often, left-hemisphere types fear any loss of control and believe they will do something "wrong," bad, or foolish. The stress of being a living computer might lead them to escape by getting drunk, thus freeing right hemisphere without any limitations. When they logically survey the results of their drunkenness, they become convinced of the danger of not being logical and acting logically. This reinforces the very belief system that prevents them from mediating their behavior and choices. We could demonstrate the same process in reverse for the individual who has escaped into right hemisphere and continues to find "proof" to support their belief system that they cannot be organized, logical or disciplined.

Now, what of the individual who falls into that category known as well-adjusted or self-actualized? (Maslow, 1975) Will they tend toward a graceful, eclectic and flexible mixture of both right hemisphere and left hemisphere? Able to make plans and then follow through? Reasonably well-organized but flexible enough to give up what doesn't work and try something new? Will they tend to use creative approaches to work and play rather than follow the same proven steps? Will they be spontaneous with a well-developed sense of humor?

You will have to look and listen for yourself until it fits for you. You may discover that these individuals have the ability to be a rational, logical adult where that is required; a happy spontaneous explorative child where that is the better choice, and both when both are most appropriate.

GOAL: HEMISPHERIC BALANCE

If, from the preceding, you have jumped to the conclusion that helping individuals to become more hemispherically balanced is your goal...you've made a good jump! Review your own history as to those areas you handle well. You will no doubt discover—as to those areas—a balance between spontaneous creativity and disciplined goal direction. Or, turning right and left at the same time.

Now, review some of your therapeutic successes in which your client/patient "got it together." It may become clear that, as those individuals moved toward their therapeutic goal, they not only broke self-defeating patterns, they also moved closer to reciprocal hemispheric utilization. In his book, *The Furthest Reaches of Human Nature,* Abraham Maslow described the self-actualized individual as the highest of achievements. Paraphrasing Maslow, he stated that the self-actualized individual has the ability to leave behind everyday reality in order to delve fully into his creative process, decide to return to reality, choose what can be and then plan to work to make it happen. If we translate this into the language of our discussion, it might be stated that the self-actualized individual has the ability to put aside left-hemisphere activity to explore fully right-hemisphere activity, and then utilize left hemisphere to bring right-hemisphere creativity to fruition. Ornstein (1972) has predicted that if each side of the brain is utilized, both sides will produce more than if only one side is used. As in the concept of synergy the sum of the parts will be more than the parts themselves.

HEMISPHERES: HYPNOSIS

Hypnosis, by its very nature, may be one of the most effective ways of helping someone toward hemispheric balance and self-actualization. Hemispheric research amply demonstrates that as an individual enters into an altered state, his right hemisphere becomes more active, while the left hemisphere rests. In such a state, right hemisphere processes become more evident and the individual finds it more acceptable to acknowledge that process. Since hypnosis is an imaginistic state that produces sensory responses (Erickson and Rossi, 1979; Kroger, 1976; Wolberg, 1964), the individual finds himself fully involved in his "other reality," thereby opening channels of communication between left and right. In most cases, the hypnotic state produces, if not a change in left-hemisphere beliefs, at least a substantial putting aside and questioning of left-hemisphere beliefs and limitations. Ask a hypnotically naive individual if they believe they could anesthetize their arm by thinking certain words. Most would express doubt. After experiencing hypnotic anesthesia, they can never again have their prior belief. All the facts in the world will not convince them so thoroughly as their awareness of their experience. Those of you who utilize hypnosis can verify that statement. Remember the surprise a subject has expressed after a hand levitation.

HEMISPHERIC AMNESIA

As stated elsewhere, chronic pain patients claim they always have pain. Since their left-hemisphere reality is one of remembering pain, where there is no pain there is nothing for them to remember. They have amnesia for no-pain (Erickson and Rossi, 1979). In the same vein, most of us have little or no left-hemisphere memory for all the ways we utilize hemispheric balance gracefully and efficaciously. Even so-called "dysfunctioning" people have such a balance in the trouble-free areas of their lives. Since their left-hemisphere reality is focused and locked into their problem where there is little or no balance, they tend to have forgotten all of their balanced areas: driving a car, riding a bicycle, reading, writing, recognizing a friend, tying shoelaces, and on and on.

It has been estimated that individuals handle at least 70–80% of life's requirements effectively. It is the 20%, 30% or, in some cases 40%, that have forgotten how to turn right and left at the same time. The hypnotic state, by its release of imaginistic recall and fantasy, can be used to help them to not only re-experience themselves using those areas of successful balance, but to also "see and feel" themselves using those skills to solve their problems. Helping an individual to "relive" learning to ride a bicycle, to read and write, to tie shoelaces—situations in which they once doubted their abilities—helps to interrupt their left-hemisphere limitations.

CASE 8: INTRODUCTION

To underscore the efficacy of hypnotic utilization, I will present a case that required just two sessions to achieve the patient's therapeutic goal. While several factors were involved in the successful outcome, the use of hypnotic fantasy and right-hemisphere memories of competency were the key elements. The patient was a recently divorced man, 30 years of age. His complaint was of being afraid to approach women; he believed he lacked the confidence to learn how. Early in the first session, he had stated, "I can't see myself approaching a woman, no way! I'm afraid I'll look foolish, and that really scares me." On a more positive note, he considered himself an excellent tennis player.

Translating his stated complaint into the language of our discussion, I would state his problem as follows: His "logical" or left-hemisphere experience and belief was that he could not be successful approaching a woman, that he "knew" he would look foolish. Individuals who over rely on left-hemispheric functions (either in general or in the problem area) tend toward strong fears of appearing foolish and tend not to use their creative imagination (right hemisphere) as a method of solving their problem. They tend to take the same facts, follow them in the same sequence and end up in the same stuck place. On the other hand, he felt good about his ability to play tennis.

Since at some point in time he was *not* skillful at tennis, he must have, in that situation at least, found a way of overcoming his fear of looking foolish. Stated in another way, within his memory banks (right-hemispheric experience) was the skill of feeling confident (at tennis) and of being able to learn something new. The task, therefore, was to help him break out of his left-hemispheric limitations and to help him utilize his right-hemisphere creative imagination to find a new way of solving his problem.

Since hypnosis results in more right-hemispheric activity while reducing the activity of the left hemisphere (getting the individual out of their own way), a combination of hypnosis and what Erickson has termed "embedded suggestion" was utilized. The purpose was to free his creative imagination, enable him to experience his (tennis) confidence, and enable him to generalize that confidence to the problem area.

CASE 8: TENNIS

The following is an edited transcript of the important elements of his two sessions:

DR: So you have confidence in your ability to play tennis?

PT: Yes! I'm really very good at it.

DR: That's great. What do you see as the best aspects of your game?

PT: My serve, my backhand and the way I move up to play the net.

DR: I have trouble moving close to the net, but you seem to be *CONFIDENT* about *MOVING IN CLOSE.* [Emphasis and caps indicate slower speech and lower tonality: In effect marking out confidence, and moving in close as a separate message.]

PT: It just takes practice.

DR: Really? [Said with doubting tone and facial expression.]

PT: Yeah, you just have to practice. [Pt. is now introducing the importance of practice himself and he is led to reinforce that by the doubt expressed by Dr.]

DR: How do you know you're confident at tennis?

PT: Huh? I don't understand.

DR: When you take a trip, say to Las Vegas, you know you've arrived when you see the bright lights and the signs; you know when you've really finished a meal when you feel full; you recognize your favorite music when you hear the melodies.

Utilizing all systems, Visual-Kinesthetic-Auditory, and beginning with visual since he had earlier stated, "I can't see myself approaching women... I'm afraid I'll look foolish." Those statements indicated that, at least in his problem area, he was stuck in his visual system—that is, he made visual pictures (V) of some future disaster with women, probably based on some prior visual learning, and then he feels (K) in response to those pictures. In effect, his internal reality became more real than his external reality.

PT: I'm not sure I see what you mean, but I guess it's a feeling I have.

DR: [Dr.'s head tilts slightly to his right, directing the next communication to the patient's left ear (RH) with slower speech and lower tonality. From this point on, emphasis and caps indicate head tilt, slower speech and lower tonality.] *THAT'S RIGHT! IT'S A FEELING!* Tell me more about that good solid feeling.

[implying that the feeling is good and solid, and of course, you can get a hold of something solid.]

PT: [Eyes move slightly up and left while he "looks" for his memory of that solid feeling; he begins to relax, and there is a noticeable change in his breathing.] I feel good... [dots indicating a pause] kinda strong... [eyes down to his right indicating a switch to his kinesthetic system, and he evidences a positive response. This helps to confirm that the source of his problem is in his visual memories and expectations.] ...There's also a sense of excitement and well-being.

DR: How do you think you look when you...*FEEL CONFIDENT?* [hidden suggestion and beginning to help patient to associate good feelings with visual images.]

PT: [Smiling] I've never looked at myself, but I guess I look sort of proud...and confident. [At this point he begins to sit up straight in the chair, squares his shoulders, and his voice takes on a strong tone, in effect showing how he looks and feels.]

DR: *THAT'S RIGHT!...* Just like you do *NOW!* [associating more pleasant experiences into his visual system] ...and when you've played a great set, and discuss it, how does your voice sound now! [mixing past experiences—"played" a great set—with the present—How "does" your voice sound "now!" In addition, beginning a positive association with his speaking.]

PT: I guess like it sounds now. [acknowledging the experience he is now having.]

DR: That's a *GREAT FEELING...NOW...*isn't it? [Dr. adds smile which will be included with tonality, head tilt, etc.]

PT: [head nodding, smiling] Yeah! I want that when I talk to a woman. [indicating he is connecting the experiences and is recognizing the potential.]

DR: But you didn't...*ALWAYS HAVE CONFIDENCE...* [unconscious suggestion] when you first started playing tennis. [reinforcing the connection between the two experiences: starting without confidence, working at it, and gaining confidence.

At this point, head tilt, etc. has become an automatic cue eliciting in the patient a positive response. In effect, an unconscious suggestion.] Did you know that fear is nothing more than *FOR...GETTING YOUR CONFIDENCE?*

The word "forgetting" above: FOR...GETTING YOUR CONFIDENCE had been said very slowly, with a slight pause between "for" and "getting." In addition to the message the patient understood conversationally, there was also an unconscious suggestion: FEAR IS FOR GETTING CONFIDENCE; i.e., use the signal of fear as a cue to remember being confident. This uses his real life expectations and experiences to help trigger a new response.

PT: [Smiling] You mean I know how to be confident, I just forget. [Indicating he is integrating the unconscious suggestion.]

DR: *THAT'S RIGHT!* [Head tilt, tonality, smile] And if you've forgotten it, you must have it somewhere. You can't forget what you haven't learned. However, in the past you have been terrified when you tried to talk to a woman. [Said with a flat, almost accusing tone and using the past, implying it was in the past only.]

PT: [Body slumping, voice quavering] Yeah, it really scared me. [Indicating he is beginning to put the fear in the past: "scared" as opposed to "scares."]

DR: [head tilt, tonality, smile] *BUT YOU KNOW HOW TO FEEL GOOD IN A SNAP.* [Snapped fingers interrupting his pattern or response while head tilt, etc. elicits the now associated good feelings.]

PT: [Holds breath, then slowly exhales, relaxes and smiles] I don't know what you're doing, but I was feeling bad and all of a sudden I feel good again.

DR: [Head tilt, tonality, smile] *THAT'S RIGHT!* [head to normal position, normal tone] A part of you knows how [pause, head tilt, etc.] TO *FEEL GOOD...WHENEVER...YOU WANT TO FEEL GOOD!*

At this point, I discussed the game of tennis in general terms with a strong emphasis on being unsure in the beginning and then, with practice, it gets easier and easier. This theme was repeated several times while discussing the skills of tennis: learning to serve, learning to have a smooth backhand, etc. Since the patient already knew all this, it was hoped he would become bored consciously, and since he knew what he wanted—confidence in regards to women—he would take the important parts of the message—practice leads to skill and confidence—and apply it to his goal. (Erickson, Rossi and Rossi, 1979) During this seemingly repetitive conversation, I began a formal induction:

DR: One of the important skills you've learned automatically to watch the ball with interest. [Improper sentence intended—read it again.] Just as you've *NOW WATCHING ME WITH INTEREST* [head and tone, no smile] to respond automatically...to the ball without thought, just as you are *BEGINNING WITH ME* [head, tone, improper sentence] holding that racquet [stated as if he were holding a racquet: leads to disassociation]. and *THAT HAND* [head tilt] had learned to *MOVE AUTOMATICALLY* as if a mind of its own [right hand makes slight motion] *JUST LIKE THAT'S RIGHT* [head tilt, running two sentences together] and I really don't know which hand will...*BEGIN TO FLOAT UP* [head tilt] to rest against your face [right hand twitches more. Long pause, 10–15 seconds] *THAT'S RIGHT* [head tilt, 10–15 seconds pause] IT IS...a pleasure to have that *UPLIFTING EXPERIENCE* [double message: it is with pause, equals it is moving, equals a pleasure, etc., equals, it is a pleasure to have that movement. Patient's hand jerks several times and slowly, with short jerking movement, begins to move up.] Your unconscious mind will decide if you will...*CLOSE YOUR EYES* while your *HAND MOVES UP...OR AS IT TOUCHES YOUR FACE.* [The above implies he has an unconscious and that it can decide, and uses the illusion of choice! His eyes will close, he has to choose when.] Consciously *YOU MAY BE SURPRISED AT WHERE YOUR HAND TOUCHES YOUR FACE...*or *I COULD BE WRONG AND YOU WONT BE SURPRISED AT ALL!* [This allows him to realize that his conscious doesn't know what his unconscious can do, and implies that he will complete the suggestion. I gave him a chance to prove me wrong. He doesn't have to be surprised at all.]

Patient's eyes blink slowly then close, he breathes deeply, facial muscles relax and he proceeds into a formal hypnotic state. His hand rises, and after several minutes touches his face and stops there.

DR: No matter how fast I want your hand to move down, I want you to fight it and do not allow it to move down any more quickly than is comfortable for you which will be no more quickly than you continue to go deeply. [Pt. hand stops against face for 3 or 4 minutes and I say softly, "That's right," two or three times in time with evidence of deepening—i.e., breathing slowly, facial muscles becoming flaccid—and then said again as hand began to move slowly down.]

The patient, through simple story form, was reminded of his acquisition of skills during his childhood: learning to ride a bike, roller skate, play sports, etc. Each story was about three minutes in length, emphasizing starting out a little afraid but wanting to learn, practicing, falling, getting up, learning, and gaining confidence. At the end of each story I said, "THAT'S RIGHT," increasing the association factor. He was told to take all the time he needed to return to conscious awareness, and that he would not return any more quickly than he needed to review one particular time of learning to be confident, and to bring those feelings with him. After nearly ten minutes, he opened his eyes.

PT: Hey, that was great. I feel good.

DR: *THAT'S RIGHT!* New learning is always interesting; but I have a problem [intentionally changing the thrust and interrupting his conscious processes] and I need your help.

PT: [blinks eyes and stares intently] What can I do?

DR: Well, therapists need what is known as base line data [some examples of such data was given]. Since I can't be inside of you to know what happened when you got scared *IN THE PAST* [head tilt, slower pace] and since we need something to judge your progress, by I have an assignment for you.

PT: OK.

DR: I want you to get a small notebook and go out and try to get rejected by five women in one week. Approach them in any acceptable way and pay close attention to your responses. [Patient begins to act a little nervous.] It's important to notice [back to visual] how you feel and see what happens to you. This will give us the information we need to help you. Of course, you can refuse, but you will look foolish asking for help and then refusing to help. [Intentionally using his fear of "looking foolish" to motivate him. In effect, a double bind. In addition, carrying out the assignment itself will require that he approach women.]

PT: Well, I don't like it, but it would be foolish to pay you and not cooperate with you.

DR: *THAT'S RIGHT!* [head tilt, tonality, eliciting his positive association to his new task] Now time is up. I'll see you next week, and with your base line data we can really get down to work.

CASE 8: SECOND SESSION

PT: [Patient appears smiling and looking excited.] Well, I didn't quite carry out my assignment. I was only able to be rejected by three women. I managed to meet six ladies and I've been out on two dates this past week. Boy, you should have seen me *LOOK-ING GOOD!* [patient's voice is strong and he looks very pleased and his report of seeing ladies and looking good indicates his visual system is now seeing positive experiences]

At this point the patient discussed how he made his first approach, his fears which began to lessen, and his growing confidence. "It just kept getting easier." Every time he felt afraid, he remembered that being scared meant he was for-getting to be confident. He also stated, with confidence, that his problem was solved.

DR: *THAT'S RIGHT!* [smile, head tilt, tonality] Now you remember how that hand began to rise up last week [patient looks at right hand, which began to twitch] You know how to enjoy that same experience NOW! [Eyes close and he enters into hypnosis.]

The balance of the hypnotic experience was regarding his tennis game to overlay his skills with meeting women; e.g.,:

DR: You are proud and confident about your serve and as you feel
         that, you can see yourself serving to a woman on the other side
         of the net, you know how to move in close to the net and handle
         whatever is hit your way, and just as you can move toward a
         woman and see yourself handling it and how off-handed you
         can be with your backhand.

Many stories equating tennis and meeting women were used to reinforce his goal. It was a good bet he would fill in. While no formal follow
up was attempted, this patient referred several people, one of whom
relayed the message that things were great and he was getting better all
the time, just like his tennis game!

XI

Reality ... Really???

CONSENSUAL REALM

Scientists who study human behavior have argued, and continue to argue, as to what constitutes "reality"; if there is a reality, why a reality, and...ad nauseam. In spite of this debate, one general consensus has come into being: There exists a "consensual reality." As the name implies, it refers to a consensus, or general agreement, as to what to call certain things and how generally we should respond to those things. We, at least in our society, generally agree that a chair is a chair, and what we can do with a chair (careful...).

We know that we can't, at least at this point in our development, flap our arms and fly. We all agree that a beach is a beach, a tree is a tree, etc. In a very narrow sense, we might state that consensual reality is primarily a function of conscious processes: that is, I see a tree and accept the object as a tree. Unless one of us is marching to a very different drummer, you would agree that a tree is just that—a tree. Thus, we have consensual agreement as to the reality of that tree. However, our individual response to that tree may be more important than our agreement.

> A tree is a tree—although its meaning to the man who views it ("the truth") depends upon his relationship to it. Does it give him fruit or shade, or is it an obstacle in his path?
> — *Surveying Kierkegaard,* Homer and Buhler, 1969

INTERNAL REALITY

Our internal (subjective) reality, and, therefore, our response to that tree may be entirely different from that of another person. This factor (internal reality) contributes to our individual uniqueness. No two people will perceive or respond to the beach in exactly the same way; no two people perceive and respond in the same way to a painting. I believe that our internal realities make for a exciting differences among all of us. If not for this "reality," we would all be gray-flannel, button-down, pin-striped people, or some other stereotype.

A man enters a room. Across the room he sees a woman. He begins to experience strong arousal and finds himself powerfully attracted to her. Now, consciously, he is only seeing certain physical characteristics: perhaps blond hair, blue eyes, a nice figure, or whatever. (Men, feel free to alter the above description, and women, fill in your own favorite fantasy.)

There may be many other women in the room, and we might consensually agree that they are all at least as attractive as that one woman. In spite of that, our hero stands there having his powerful experience, and is almost oblivious to the other women. In all probability, he is unaware that in his inner reality, he is responding to a whole past history of unconscious associations. Perhaps her hair is the same as his first puppy love; her lips are like those of the first girl he ever kissed; her smile is that of the first woman he ever had sex with. In "reality" he is not responding to her at all. In effect, "seeing" her caused him to regress through his history and past experiences with women, and his inner "reality" then became more "real" and important than his outer or consensual reality.

Within his consensual reality, there is no knowledge of that woman, who she is, what she likes or is like; in fact, she may have a personality he can't stand. In spite of all that, he is standing there—his heart beating rapidly, his palms sweating, his mind locked totally on her—while he is desperately trying to figure out ways of meeting her. You might...*NOW ASK YOURSELF*...which reality is real...at least for him?

Everything we see, feel, hear and "know" is tempered, perceived, filtered and responded to based on our internal belief systems (see Chapter V). The way we have learned to see, interpret and respond is individual for each of us. The unconscious mind's "inner reality" may be entirely different from that of our conscious mind's consensual "reality." In his work, *The Split Brain in Man,* Gazzaneza (1967) touched lightly on this topic when he stated, "...it is as if the cranium contained two separate spheres of consciousness."

MONSTERS AND MAGICAL STICKS

When my son was about three or four, he decided that his baseball and football became monsters at night when the lights were turned off. He "saw" them coming to life; they looked evil and they were trying to get him. Now, rationally, that makes no sense at all. Our consensual reality knows that it's not real. My wife and I attempted to explain to him what was real and what was not. He listened very intently and when we finished, he said, "But they're coming to get me." For whatever the reasons, his unconscious mind had created this inner reality, and it had suddenly leaped out to become his outer reality. Logical, factual, linear, left-hemispheric explanations accomplished the sum total of nothing.

We then decided to become illogical (some might call it creative) to solve the problem. We went to a local building supply store and obtained a piece of wood doweling, two feet long and one-half inch in diameter. We wrapped the dowel in purple velvet and put a little gold tassel at one end. Next we purchased the kind of box one would put roses into and placed the soon to be "magic stick" inside. We brought the box home and explained to our son that we had been to see a special doctor called the magic doctor. We told him that the magic doctor had made a magic stick that would scare away all monster balls. We then told him the "magic" words that the magic doctor had given us. We explained to him that for two or three nights he was to point the magic stick at the monster and say the magic words.

That night we all went into his bedroom and went through a solemn ceremony of opening the box and presenting him with the magic stick. He took the stick and, with great determination, went around the room. At each corner of the room he stopped, pointed the magic stick and said the magic words. That night he slept without his previous nightmares and sudden awakenings. The second night, he went into his room alone and repeated the magic ritual. After the third or fourth night, he put the magic stick in a corner and stopped using it. He slept without problems and no longer talked about monsters.

About two weeks later he gave us the stick and said he no longer needed it. The moral of this story is: Since his unconscious processes, based on his belief systems, created his inner reality of monster balls, it took his unconscious processes to create an inner reality that believed in a cure more powerful than the monster balls to solve the problem. Traditional approaches would have entailed reasoning it out and proving that the monster balls did not exist, or "plumbed" the depth of his feelings; or helped (?) him to act out his (pick one) fears/angers/hostilities/insecurities. Then, in several months (or years), he would have been able to cope with *"The Problem."* Instead, within a matter of a few days, he not only learned *how* to solve the problem...he *had solved it.*

CRAZINESS AND CREATIVITY

To me, the unconscious mind and its inner reality is a fascinating, creative, dynamic and exciting place. It has been said that the unconscious process is similar to that of the schizophrenic process. I believe, however, that the so-called schizophrenic process, directed toward the solving of problems and the discovery of that which is new, is the *creative process.* This same process, turned toward building limitations and fears, can be called "craziness." To paraphrase George Santayana: Creativity is merely craziness put to good use.

Another personal story might make the point even more clear. Many years ago, we lived on the second floor of a two-story apartment building. My daughter, who was three at the time, had developed the habit of jumping off her bed over and over, playing some private game that only she understood. One night, our downstairs neighbor came up to complain about the noise. My wife went into our daughter's room and said, "Don't do that anymore. The man downstairs is getting very angry." Later that night our daughter became very upset. When we tried to calm her down, she told us that the man who lived in the rug was mad at her and was going to hurt her. We attempted to explain the concept of upstairs/downstairs, but she was too young to understand. We even took her downstairs to show her where the man "down below" lived. All she could or would understand was that the man in the carpeting was mad at her for jumping on him.

Now, we adults know that's ridiculous. We adults, we who think logically, know that a man can't live in the carpet. We logical adults who throw salt over our shoulder, who knock on wood when we have good fortune, who step around ladders and step over cracks, know that those little childish beliefs have nothing to do with us. (That's why this book has no Chapter 13. Reality ... Really?)

IMAGES OF REALITY

As we stated earlier, when a patient enters the therapist's office, he brings with him his inner belief systems: a process of his past learnings, experiences, and individual realities. This individual lives in basically the same outer reality as the therapists and has many of the same opportunities. However, that person's inner reality may be such that he is blocked from seeing the opportunities and options that are available. In effect, s/he has been hypnotized, or has hypnotized him/herself, into seeing that which s/he has already seen, hearing only what s/he has already heard, and feeling only that which s/he has already felt.

...let us remember. We never deal with reality per se, but rather with images of reality—that is, with interpretations. While the number of potentially possible interpretations is very large, our world image permits us to see only one—and this one therefore appears to be the only possible, reasonable, and permitted view. Furthermore, this one interpretation also suggests only one possible reasonable and permitted solution, and if we don't succeed at first, we try and try again—or, in other words, we resort to the recipe of doing more of the same.

— Watzlawick, 1978, p. 119

The therapist who insists on attacking the patient's belief systems directly is using a hammer as her only tool, and will, as a result, treat the patient as if he were a nail! Since there could well be an inner reality of jumping off a bed and causing the man who lives in the carpet to get angry, attacking the patient's belief system directly is not, in most cases, going to help. It may even hurt and result in that great escape clause...*RESISTANCE*...

Devising an unconscious process that uses the same creativity that *produced* the problem to *solve* the problem will be a much more effective approach. In addition, it's a lot more fun for the therapist as well as the patient.

HYPNOTIC MONSTER

A woman who suffered from severe anxiety whenever she was in a relationship with a man, sought my help. She described her reaction as a feeling of drowning, or suffocating, and claimed she actually experienced those sensations physically. She had been working on her problem for just over two years, and had, in her opinion, made good progress. She "understood" the dynamics, had insight, and felt stronger in handling the "bad" feelings. She believed that she was now ready to get rid of the problem once and for all.

She acknowledged that her problem made no sense "logically." She had read extensively on the subjects of psychology, therapy, and interpersonal relationships. In spite of her efforts, she felt stuck and said, "I'm beginning to lose all hope." During her second session I helped her into the state that doesn't exist—hypnosis. I asked her to "go back" to a time when she had experienced those bad feelings and to signal me by raising the first finger of her left hand when she could actually feel the sensations. After she signaled, and was evidencing some discomfort, I told her to allow her creative mind to create a horrible monster, to see it clearly, and to feel all the fear as it was trying to destroy her.

She was then asked to imagine that there was no safe path of escape. Within a few moments, there were obvious signs of discomfort: her breathing rate increased dramatically, sweat appeared on her forehead and upper lip, and she was evidencing agitation. At that point, I told her the following: "It's up to you to decide whether to knock your monster out, or to wiggle your nose and chase it away, or to flap your ears and simply fly away and leave the monster where it belongs—in the past. Now, take your time, because your unconscious mind may want to use a combination of those things, or it may have even better ways."

Now, we all know that not one of those instructions makes sense logically, and yet, in spite of the nonsense, something began to happen. Within a few moments, she took a few deep breaths and exhaled very slowly; her body began to relax and then she started to giggle. Five minutes later she opened her eyes and smiled a beautiful smile. She told me that, for some reason, she knew that she didn't have to be afraid anymore, that she didn't understand it, but somehow she had a "gut" feeling where the monster came from and how to get rid of it.

THE SNOWMAN AS REALITY

When my daughter was about four years old, my wife and I took her to see snow for the first time. She wanted to build a snowman, and we helped her to build one that was "little people" size—about two and a half feet tall. She was very excited and pleased with her creation, and we were pleased, too. As we drove into our driveway, after returning from the mountains, she saw several of her friends playing. She asked me to stop the car so she could get out and tell them about the snowman. She got out and excitedly began to tell them all about her snowman.

As she described it, she painted a picture with her hands that made the snowman about four feet high. She had almost doubled its height. Two days later we all went to breakfast with my parents. Our daughter began to describe her snowman and said, "Grandpa, I made a snowman bigger than you." My father is about 5'10", and at the time, quite a bit overweight. That started me to think about how our imaginations work: To a child, if they are not right there to see it, a snowman gets bigger and bigger. If that's true of a snowman, what about those monsters we built when we were children? They were no more than six inches tall, but while we have been running from them all these years, I bet our inner reality has made them forty-seven feet tall, and very, very scary.

Since our creative unconscious has built our monsters so big, our creative unconscious knows just how to wiggle our nose and reduce the monster to size. But, that's just a different reality... Really!

XII

Unconscious Versus Conscious

Among my many pet peeves, one stands out: Many people who utilize hypnosis, as well as therapists of all types, will pay lip service to the existence of a so-called "unconscious." They will discuss unconscious processes, unconscious problems, and unconscious conflicts. Yet, when it comes to doing therapy, they act as if the unconscious doesn't exist. You could safely say that they are unconscious as to unconscious processes.

They will attempt to explain to their patients, in specific, logical detail, just what the problem and its solution is. Unless they are dealing with someone from another planet, their patient has probably heard all the logical advice they could give. The patient has probably heard "the answer" from many sources. If these "facts" were the solution, I'm sure they would have solved their problem:

> Once upon a time, there was a young woman and a young man crawling around on their hands and knees. They seemed to be searching desperately for something. A kind and well-meaning stranger happened by and asked them, "What are you looking for?" They replied, "We are searching for some important keys that will unlock important doors in our lives." The stranger said, "That sounds important. Let me help you look." The stranger got down on his/her hands and knees and began searching for the missing keys. After a long while, the stranger stopped and said, "I can't find any keys here... Just where were you standing when you lost them?" The couple replied, "Oh, about one hundred miles from here, in an open field." The stranger said, "If you lost them in a field one hundred miles from here, what are we doing searching here?" "Well," said the couple, "the light is very good here, and we already know the territory perfectly." — Old Sufi tale, updated a little

SUB. VS. UNCONSCIOUS

Some individuals prefer the concept of a *subconscious* mind. I prefer the concept of the *unconscious*. According to the American Heritage Dictionary (Dell Publishing Inc., 1975), the prefix "sub" implies lesser than, beneath or below instead of parallel or equal. I like to believe that the "two minds" are equal, but different. In the most basic terms, I believe that unconscious mind means that of which we are not (at least for the moment) *conscious*. There are a multitude of processes that we become aware of (conscious) at different times and circumstances. There are many more (processes) that we may never, or only seldom, become conscious of. In spite of this lack of "awareness," these processes are there and ongoing.

For example, as you are reading these words, your heart has been beating. Until you read that statement, you were probably unconscious as to that process. Some of you may have difficulty experiencing that process now. But, since you are reading this book, I am assuming that you are alive and, therefore, that process is continuing.

"THE PSYCHOLOGICAL UNCONSCIOUS"

A few years ago, a research paper was published regarding the subject of unconscious processes. The gist of this paper was, that by flashing words on a screen at a high rate of speed—euphemistically called "subliminally"—the subjects would evidence physiological responses without conscious awareness of the words. One experiment included the flashing of sexually stimulating material in the midst of a very "dry" intellectual movie, again at a speed that prevented the subjects from being "aware" of the material. Yet, all of the subjects gave evidence of strong "physiological arousal." (Scientists must have difficulty saying turned on.)

The researchers, based on the results of these and other so-called "subliminal experiments," concluded that there is an unconscious process. They further concluded that not only are these (unconscious) processes occurring at all times, but we are most often unaware of not only the process, but how the process affects us. Howard Shevrin and Scott Dickman, in their paper, "The Psychological Unconscious" stated, "...unconscious processes affect ongoing behavior and experience, even though the experiencer may be unaware of this influence." *(American Psychologist,* 1980, Vol. 35, Number 5, 421–434.)

Dr. Milton Erickson, who has insisted for years that there is an unconscious process, upon hearing about the above "discovery" said, (this is a paraphrase), "I'm not surprised that the scientific community is finally acknowledging the existence of the unconscious. What does surprise me is that they still insist that there is a conscious mind!" There are some mind/brain researchers who claim that so-called conscious reality is really a gift from our unconscious mind; that is, only when our unconscious mind makes our conscious mind aware of something, does that something become part of our reality.

A LIE

What you are now about to read is a lie! I believe that it will be a useful lie. If you will recall the material from Chapter X, "Left Meets Right Meets Left," it was pointed out that the two hemispheres of the brain specialize. To recap briefly, the left, or so-called dominant, hemisphere deals with linear, digital, analytical and logical processes. The right hemisphere's domain is spatiality, imagery, color perception, kinesthetic recall, and creativity; it may be called the metaphoric mind.

I would like you to...*ACCEPT NOW*...the lie that the left hemisphere may be conceptualized as the conscious mind, while the right hemisphere is the home of the unconscious mind. If you accept this untruth, you will be in very good company. There are many mind/brain researchers and scientists who accept, and even spread, this lie. They might even say that what we call unconscious processes match nicely with what is known about right-hemispheric activity, and ditto for conscious processes/left hemisphere. Technically, it might be more accurate to state that both hemispheres engage in unconscious and conscious processes, and that neither hemisphere works totally independently of the other. Rather, there is a consistent interaction and interchange between the two. In referring to the "location" of the consciousness and memory, Buzan and Dixon (cited) stated:

> It becomes clear in fact, that such elusive phenomena were in some way distributed throughout the brain as a whole.... However, some researchers of brain phenomena now make a distinction between mind and brain in what is termed the mind/brain dualism. If, in fact, such a dualism exists, scientists are not yet close to identifying where one starts and the other leaves off.

Remember, I said that what you were going to read is a lie—so the above may be a lie also!

UNCONSCIOUS/CONSCIOUS/METAPHOR

While a separate left hemisphere/conscious mind and a right hemisphere/unconscious mind may or may not exist, I find it a useful metaphor for my work with hypnosis. When engaged in so-called "conscious work," I use facts, logic, and reason. When I move to "doing hypnosis," I use stories, imaginistic recall, nonsense suggestions and fantasy—in short, "the language of the unconscious."

I also accept that the two "minds" work in concert—when not working in opposition. For example, you consciously see an individual standing on a street corner. Your unconscious mind takes the total picture and goes through its file cabinet of memories, and comes up with a recognition. This recognition is then sent to your conscious mind and you "recognize" a friend you haven't seen in years.

An example we have all experienced: We are introduced to someone new. Several hours later we try to recall their name, but to no avail. We have "forgotten." We struggle for a while and then say, "To hell with it." Later, as we are busy at some other task, the name suddenly "pops" into our (conscious) mind. We weren't even aware of the process of remembering. This is a simple, but descriptive, example of one unconscious process. However, there are many other unconscious processes that may not be so innocuous. They may even be painful.

UNCONSCIOUS PROTECTION

Dr. Milton Erickson has steadfastly contended that the unconscious always protects the conscious and the total organism. While I would agree in general, I would add an important corollary. The unconscious always protects the individual the best way it "knows" how, within the framework of its reality, and the rules followed by the conscious mind and its reality.

The methods of the unconscious may have once been useful, or may have been the best choice available at another time, or the best "allowed" at another time. That is no guarantee that its "protection" is in the individual's *present* best interest! In other situations, the unconscious may have "a better method," but the belief systems of the conscious mind may deny, block or ignore the message of the unconscious.

I belief that, where the unconscious does not have an easy channel of communication to the conscious mind, or where its messages are denied or ignored, it will find a way to make itself known. Symptomology (physical or emotional) may be one such group of ways. Where reciprocal communication between the two "minds" is severed via the surgeries of past traumas, past learning, fears about "losing control," etc., will that be where the unconscious is "forced" to sneak into the picture for the purpose of "rearranging" the pieces of that individual's puzzle? Will the conscious mind push the intruder away? Will the individual find himself responding in ways that are not acceptable to his conscious understanding? Will that lead to anxiety? Will that lead to more conscious control and denial of the unconscious message? Will that result in the unconscious increasing its efforts to "protect" by becoming more insistent?

SYMPTOM: TENSION HEADACHE

For a possible answer to the above questions, we need only examine the symptom known as tension headache. Most medical experts would agree that, in the absence of physical pathology, such headaches occur from impaired circulation and building pressure when increasing muscle tension is ignored. I would like you to consider this causative chain of events from the metaphoric concept of Right Hemisphere/Left Hemisphere—Conscious/Unconscious processes.

You have been hard at work at some task, and without your "awareness" your mind and body are tired. Your unconscious recognizes your need for a work break, and it "communicates" this information through one of its languages: i.e., kinesthetic signals. Your back and neck tighten up. You either ignore or are unaware of the message, and so you continue to work. Your unconscious, in its effort to "protect" you, increases its message. The message gets stronger; more tightness affecting more of your body, and then...*HEADACHE!* You can't concentrate, your eyes ache, your head pounds, and you are forced to take a break—which is what your unconscious wanted in the first place. You could say that an individual's unconscious, under the right conditions, could even make them crazy in order to protect them. I hope that the following two brief case histories will be useful in underlining the message.

CASE 9: HEADACHE

A man was referred to me who had a long history of so-called tension headaches. He averaged three to four severe headaches a day. He tended to be a compulsive individual in all of his activities, but more so when it came to "keeping on top of my work." I asked him to imagine the following: that he had a very urgent message for a friend, and that he went to his friend's house to deliver it. He knew his friend was home, so he rang the doorbell but no one answered. I asked him what he would do, assuming the message had to be delivered. He replied that he would push the doorbell and hold it, and if that didn't work, he would pound on the door and shout his friend's name.

I asked him to consider that his unconscious had an important message for him, tried knocking on his "door" and, when he didn't answer, his unconscious then started to pound...*HEADACHE!* He was then asked to close his eyes and let his creative imagination produce a clear picture of that part of him that was sending the message, and to signal me when he had done so. He was then instructed to "ask" that part what signal would be acceptable for him to acknowledge. That part told him to respond to tension in the neck. I then suggested that he become more aware of that signal and, as soon as he felt that message, he was to stop, take several deep breaths, and then take a 10 to 15 minute break. I asked him to ask that part if that method would be acceptable, and if it was, it would be time for him to return to my office. (Somehow during these procedures, he had entered into what looked a lot like a hypnotic state.)

He opened his eyes about ten minutes later and said, "It said 'yes,' but if I don't keep my promise, it reserves the right to give me a headache." This simple procedure resulted in an 80% reduction of his symptoms within two weeks. He was then helped, while in the hypnotic state, to become more aware of his kinesthetic signals in general, and to take more frequent breaks. Within six weeks he was symptom free and has remained so. In addition, he reported that his work performance improved.

CASE 10: BEE PHOBIA

A woman complained of the following problem: About six months prior to seeing me she had developed an almost phobic response to the buzzing of bees. She told me, "They're starting to drive me crazy." After establishing what is known in the "trade" as an "anchor of comfort" (anchors are explained in Chapters XVI), I had her hold on to the feeling of comfort while she "saw" a bee at a safe distance. I asked her to then hear the buzzing while she held on to the feeling of comfort, and to listen to the sound as it changed into words; that the words would tell her what it was that her unconscious was trying to tell her.

After about fifteen minutes, she opened her eyes and said, "I'm not surprised." She told me that the bee slowly turned into her husband who was always correcting her and putting her down; and that his voice was just like the sound of a bee. (Remember, this is her unconscious process, even if it was different than I had instructed.) She went on to tell me that she was very unhappy in her marriage, but she tried to "pretend everything is great." I explained to her that she could fool some of the people all the time, and all the people some of the time, but that she couldn't fool her unconscious for even a moment. She told me that she was afraid that the "buzzing" would drive her crazy. I told her to give some thought about talking to her husband about her dissatisfaction, and even to consider marriage counseling. She called me a week later to tell me that the buzzing no longer concerned her; that as soon as she had talked to her husband, she could feel the fear "fall away."

WILD CLAIMS

For at least 150 years, hypnotists have been making wild, unscientific and unsupported claims regarding hypnosis, conscious and unconscious processes. They have claimed that the rules governing unconscious behavior and responses are different from those that control conscious processes: ("...unconscious processes may follow different principles of organization than those that characterize psychological processes occurring during the normal, waking state of consciousness." (Shevrin and Dickman, 1980).

These old time hypnotists developed what later became known as the "elevator theory": entering into hypnosis causes the unconscious to rise above the conscious and to become more active; while in the waking state, the conscious is at the higher level. Work on the 90 minute cycle of the brain and experiments with subliminal communication tends to substantiate that wild theory. Old time hypnotists held that the unconscious was always "paying attention" and "knew" everything that was going on. Shevrin and Dickman have synthesized many works that support that claim. Many surgeons are now taught that, while the patient may be "out cold," they may still record what is said in the surgery theater. Many hypnotists have had the experience of taking a subject back, while in hypnosis, to a surgery, and having the subject recall what was said. Milton Erickson has claimed that you can communicate to the unconscious separately from the conscious. His method was via stories, metaphors and talking to one ear for unconscious communication and the other ear for conscious messages.

Another wild claim by a hypnotist...and yet... "generally, subjects are unaware of the stimuli in the unattended ear, although these stimuli exercise an influence on various response parameters of the attended stimuli." (Shevrin and Dickman). Hypnotists have held that the unconscious is the storehouse of our entire history and experience; the root of our problems as well as the source of the solutions. Modern research, scientific instruments, and empirical observation have begun to prove how often those old time hypnotists were right on target. We might say that they knew how to turn left and right at the same time.

In my opinion, our highly structured society relies far too much on the logical, digital conscious part of our experience, and far too little on the creative unconscious experience. Some brain theorists have estimated that the conscious mind is capable of doing three to five unimportant tasks at one time, and only one or two important ones. At the same time, they estimate that the unconscious is capable of doing several thousand tasks at the same time.

I'm not claiming that the conscious mind is not important. What I do claim is that the average individual has a well-developed conscious mind and an under-utilized unconscious—that is, we have been trained (some might say "hypnotized") to ignore or depreciate its processes. It's as if we have exercised and developed a powerful right arm while allowing the left arm to wither. Too often, a person finds a therapist who designs an "exercise program" to further develop the "right arm" while hoping that osmosis will take care of the left one.

If, as many brain researchers claim, we use only 10% of our brain consciously, and the other 90% unconsciously, then it might be helpful to picture a pyramid. If you step back and look, you will see that a pyramid has a broad base and tapers to a narrow top. It is well-constructed to withstand stress and time. If you will picture the same pyramid upside down, you will see a structure that will have a hard time standing up. It would no doubt fall from its own weight. If you could then "see" that many people seem to use their minds as if they were upside down pyramids, then you can easily get hold of the why they topple so easily. However, let me again remind you, that I said that what you would be reading is a lie. So, too, may be that last sentence.

XIV

Utilizing Utilization

HYPNOSIS: MAGIC WORKS

In an earlier chapter, I made the statement that being a good hypnotist meant utilizing certain tools and skills that helped to direct the individual toward their own resources...and then...get the hell out of their way! My experience has been, however, that most hypnotists consistently get in the individual's way and *prevent* the hypnotic state. Therapists, in their attempt to learn the "right" way of inducing the hypnotic state, go from one hypnosis seminar to another, and from one magic book to another, in order to get "THE MAGIC WORDS" that will *make* people go into a hypnotic state. They write "THE MAGIC WORDS" down, memorize them, and attempt to hypnotize everyone with those words. When their patients/clients "refuse" to cooperate, these therapists get discouraged and either give up using hypnosis, or buy more "MAGIC BOOKS" and attend more seminars to find "THE *REAL* MAGIC WORDS." In short, these "hypnotists" are attempting to bend the patient/client to fit the mold, instead of designing the molds that will fit the patient/client.

In my opinion, producing the hypnotic state is easier than falling off the proverbial log, and much less painful. Not only does each individual already "know" how to go into hypnosis, they probably experience that state several times each day. The hypnotic state itself, as well as hypnotic phenomena, are no more, and no less, than normal occurrences and behaviors isolated, exaggerated and "spotlighted." At my training seminars (Clinical Hypnosis: Innovative Techniques®), I have often observed individuals "escaping" into their own hypnotic state to avoid the state that the "trainee hypnotist" is attempting to produce. The trainee is so busy doing it his way, that he fails to notice that his subject (victim) has "escaped." I hope, in this chapter, to share with you the attitude and skills that will enable you to achieve "that state" with more individuals more easily.

Every individual carries with him a set of learned skills, responses, attitudes and belief systems, as well as a preferred "system" (Visual—Kinesthetic—Auditory). To me, it makes far more sense to utilize these factors rather than trying to force the individual into responding according to *your* belief systems, responses, etc. By learning to utilize what the individual already knows, you will be starting from a solid foundation instead of from a morass of quicksand.

For the purpose of clarification, I would like to give a brief example. I would like you to focus on "systems" (Visual—Kinesthetic—Auditory) for a few moments. As a rule, hypnotists who are highly visual will tend to use visual induction methods—that is, they attempt to produce the hypnotic state via visual imagery. Those hypnotists who are highly kinesthetic will tend to rely on kinesthetic inductions; i.e., you're getting heavier and heavier, etc. Auditory hypnotists will tend to rely on "sounds" as an induction method. If the individual you are working with happens to match your system, you have a very good chance of being successful. If that individual doesn't "match," you can always label the lack of results as "resistance."

VISUAL INDUCTION

During one training seminar, the "hypnotist" was telling the "subject" to "feel the weight of your body, and your legs, as everything gets heavier and heavier, and you are getting more and more deeply relaxed." It sounded great—only the "subject" was not responding. The "hypnotist" said to me, "She is fighting me. Would you tell her to cooperate?" I asked her (the subject) what she thought was wrong. She replied, "I can't *seem* to get it. If he would *show* me what he means, I'll cooperate!" I asked her if she had ever gone to the beach as a child and had her legs buried in the sand. Her eyes went up left, she smiled, and looked back at me and said, "Sure." I then asked her to look across the room and see herself at the beach as a little girl. After a moment she nodded and continued to "look across the room." I then asked her to "see that little girl having her legs buried in that nice warm sand." She began staring intently and then slowly nodded her head. I said, "Good.

Now...as you see yourself floating into that picture, you can continue to remember these feelings, and then close your eyes and enjoy all of it." Within a second her eyes closed, her breathing rate slowed, and she stayed like that for several minutes. When she opened her eyes she said, "That was great! I could even smell the beach and I seem to be much more relaxed."

In the above example, the woman went from "resistance" to responding by simply allowing her to use her system (V) instead of attempting to make her use the "hypnotist's" system (K). Now, don't jump to conclusions. This example is only the tip of a very interesting iceberg. While matching systems is an important part of utilization, it is only a small part. As you continue now to read and learn, I know that you will soon discover how to utilize any and all parts of the individual's behavior to achieve the desired destination. It is my intention to cite several examples of how I have utilized utilization, and to give a brief explanation.

EXAMPLE I:

A 27-year-old woman said she had been to several hypnotists, but they couldn't hypnotize her. I asked her what she thought was preventing her from entering into hypnosis. She explained that they had all asked her to relax, but that she was always uptight (which was evidenced by her general body posture, as well as almost constant jaw clenching). She said that the more she tried to relax, the more uptight and upset she would become. When she finished her explanation, I smiled, shook my head, and said "Hey, if you knew how to relax that easily, you probably wouldn't be going to see a hypnotist." She laughed and replied, "You're right! I hadn't thought of it that way."

I then asked her to close her eyes, concentrate on her tension and to really feel all of it. After a short time she was instructed to really feel the tension in her arms and shoulders and, for the moment, *forget* the other areas, and to nod when she had done so. Within several seconds she nodded, and I said, "Now, I would like you to allow that creative part of you to give you a clear picture of what those tense muscles look like. I know that sounds strange, but that part of you can surprise you soon." When she nodded after about one minute, I asked her to keep her eyes closed while she described the picture she was seeing. (At this point, there was a noticeable reduction of her jaw clenching, and her breathing rate had slowed and deepened.)

She described the tense muscles as looking "like pink and red thick rope with big knots every few inches." I told her that she was doing great, and then asked her to allow that part of her that remembers the feelings of relaxation to give her a *clear picture* of what "those" relaxed muscles would look like. After a short time she said, "They look like big pink spaghetti, only the pink is a softer color than before." She was then asked to repeat the procedure, next with her legs—*forgetting* the arms— then her stomach area—*forgetting* the other areas—and to do it all in her own mind without talking. As she carried out her instructions, her breathing rate continued to slow, and she began to evidence a degree of physical relaxation. After nearly 20 minutes, she opened her eyes (slowly, and with some effort) and said, "That was interesting. What next?" I pointed out that our time was up, which thoroughly surprised her.

When she arrived for her next appointment, she was smiling, which was a considerable change from her first arrival. She told me that she "thought" that she had been less tense during the past week, and that her husband said that she had seemed calmer. While she wasn't sure if she had been less tense, she was sure that she was sleeping much better. (She also evidenced a substantial reduction in her general jaw-clenching behavior.) I asked her to close her eyes so that we could continue with what we had started. As soon as she closed her eyes, there was an almost instant slowing of her breathing. I instructed her to pick out one area of tension, to concentrate on feeling all of it, to get a picture of that area, and to see if the picture had changed.

After several minutes, she opened her eyes and said, "Well, it's still ropes with knots, but the knots look looser." "Like you've been feeling," I replied. I asked her to close her eyes again, and to get the picture of the knotted rope, and to signal by raising her left hand a few inches for "yes," which she did. I then said, "You have learned to get a picture from your feelings. Now, I would like you to continue your 'learnings' by getting a feeling from a picture. Ask that part of you that remembers how to relax...*NOW*...to give you a clear picture of your relaxed muscles. When you've accomplished that, you know how to signal 'yes.'"

When she signaled (raised her left hand a few inches) I said, "Now keep on watching while that part continues to help you get that relaxed feeling, and that part will signal 'yes' when she's ready. You may be surprised that when you signal 'yes,' that hand [at this point I brush her left hand lightly] will be so relaxed that it may want to float up toward your face. I must confess that I have no idea just where that hand will come to rest against your face. I will have to rely on that creative part of you to decide for both of us." Within a few minutes, not only did she look as if she was "in that state," but in addition, her left had begun a slow ascent to her face.

EXAMPLE I: DISCUSSION

This woman presented one very well-developed skill—that of being tense. There are those who might argue that tension is not a skill. On reflection, I know that they will recognize that tension, under the appropriate circumstances, would be an appropriate response. This individual, however, had lost her ability to have choice as to when to use this skill. Rather than attempt to make her conform to my blueprint, I decided to use hers. When I made the statement, "Hey, if you knew how to relax that easily, etc." I was signaling acceptance of her blueprint, being on her side, and establishing rapport all at the same time. Her response indicated that this had been successful.

By asking her to *feel* the tension, I was utilizing what she was already an expert at, thereby insuring that she would be successful, and beginning the processes of indirect suggestion. By directing her as to which area to "feel" first, I was helping her to further accept my direction. Having her "see" what the tense muscles looked like was, in fact, the first step in helping her to disassociate: Tension = Kinesthetic = Changing Kinesthetic to Visual = disconnecting or disassociating from the feeling (tension). Asking her to allow "that part" that "remembers" the feelings of relaxation, etc., was a series of unconscious communications (suggestions): 1) There was another part of her than the one she was used to; 2) That somewhere in time she had been relaxed; 3) She could remember that feeling.

When I asked her to close her eyes at the beginning of the second session, she immediately altered her rate of breathing, which indicated that she had "made the connection" and was learning to relax. By asking her to signal by raising her left hand slowly for "yes," I was setting up ideomotor response, and structuring the beginning of a possible hand levitation. (Stroking her hand lightly equals kinesthetic reinforcement of the verbal suggestion.) Since she had evidenced her ability to generate visual experiences from kinesthetic experiences, helping her to generate kinesthetic experiences from visual experiences was simply utilizing what she "knew" how to do, but redirecting it. By utilizing her "skills," "beliefs" and "systems" (Visual—Kinesthetic—Auditory), she not only achieved what she had been unable to achieve before (the hypnotic state), she also gained the ability to "picture" away her tension. As a result, her jaw clenching "got lost" and she became a much calmer individual in general.

EXAMPLE 2:

During one of the Clinical Hypnosis: Innovative Techniques® training seminars, I had asked the participants to practice a mirror/feedback induction. This induction method requires the "hypnotist" to copy the physical position and gestures of the "subject" and to verbally feed back to the subject what the subject is doing. Next, the "hypnotist" begins to slowly lead the "subject" to the desired state. As I observed the practice session, I noticed something interesting happening within one group. The "hypnotist" and the "subject" were in perfect synchronization, and each was staring intently at the other. I walked over to the group and heard the "hypnotist" saying "and now you can close your eyes." The "subject" kept staring without blinking, her breathing was very deep and she was totally still. After a few moments, the "hypnotist" said, "Well, whenever you want to you can close your eyes." The "subject" continued staring. Since they were mirroring each other so well, and since the "subject" was "locked on" to the "hypnotist," I could assume that he had done a good job of setting the stage. Yet, the "subject" would not respond to the "hypnotist's" suggestion of closing her eyes.

I positioned myself so that I was within the subject's field of vision. (I was standing while the practice group were all seated.) After a few moments, I moved my right hand up slowly, starting at my waist and ending at my cheek. As my hand moved up, the subject's eyes shifted and followed my hand as it moved up. When her eyes met mine, I nodded twice, very slowly. As she continued to stare at me, I very slowly blinked twice, nodded twice again, and then closed my eyes for three or four seconds. When I opened my eyes, the subject closed hers, and I said, "That's right! Now take all the time you need to see yourself at some pleasant place, while you continue to more deeply relax. Then go wherever you need to discover some skill or problem-solving ability that will be useful in your life... Now! When that creative part of you understands how to use those skills in your present and future situations, it will be time to return here. Be sure to bring all those good feelings back to now with you."

When the subject had first shifted her eyes to mine, the "hypnotist" looked quickly at me, then back at the subject. After I had given the verbal suggestions to the subject, I said to the hypnotist, "Since you have been watching and following her so carefully, you already know what to do." With that, I placed my fingers gently on his eyelids. His eyes closed, his body relaxed, and I said, "You heard what I asked her to do, and now you can do the exact same thing differently...in your own way." After nearly ten minutes, the man opened his eyes, and a few seconds later the woman opened hers. They looked at each other and both began to giggle. (You might say that they were continuing to mirror each other.)

EXAMPLE 2: DISCUSSION

While there was no way I could know what the woman's (subject's) general favored system was, I could see that she was staring without blinking. That indicated that, at that moment, she was into her visual system. Since they (subject and hypnotist) were matching each other, I could also assume that the man had done an excellent job of leading her to an altered state of some kind, but that he was now "in her way." He was in her way by giving her verbal instructions to do one thing (close her eyes) while he was "showing" her something else (he was staring). Since she was, at that point, into a totally visual (altered) state, she was, in fact, responding...to what she was seeing. By directing her to my eyes, I could then "show" her what was expected. To restate the above in terms of utilization, I utilized her state (visual) and used her state to lead her to the state I desired. As for the "hypnotist," the same utilization applied. Since he had been staring and matching and responding to her, when she closed her eyes, he was ready to follow. I merely gave him a "nudge."

ADDITIONAL COMMENT

Many people who engage in the practice of hypnosis, and almost all beginning hypnotists, have been hypnotized into believing that the hypnotic state requires eye closure. That is not the case! Most people, and perhaps all people, can enter into or be in a hypnotic state with their eyes wide open. There are some experts in the field of hypnosis who contend that eye closure simply makes the subject's tasks (whatever they may be) easier to accomplish. While I would agree in general, there are exceptions to that "rule."

I have worked with many people who respond better with their eyes open. In some cases, eye closure actually stops the individual from processing and responding. I believe that most hypnotists require eye closure for *their* comfort. I have observed dozens of hypnotists become "unglued" as a result of a subject staring at them. All the signs of a satisfactory hypnotic state may be present, yet the hypnotist interrupts the subject's state because "being watched" disturbs them. I hope you will learn to accept the subject's right to enter hypnosis with open eyes, and to utilize that situation as just another choice.

EXAMPLE 3:

While giving a lecture/demonstration at a local university for a group of dentists and their assistants, the following occurred: One dentist stood up and said, "While I try to use some hypnosis in my practice, I can't be hypnotized myself. I think my patients sense my failure and as a result I'm not very successful with hypnosis." I inquired as to what would transpire when he was the "subject." He said that he could feel himself fighting it, and that he would just tense up. He also stated that he didn't like anyone trying to control him. When we later moved from the lecture area into the dental clinic section, he asked me if I would "try" to hypnotize him. I asked him what hypnotic phenomena he would need to experience in order to be satisfied. He replied, "Anesthesia in some part of my body."

I asked him to take a seat in a dental chair, which he did. I picked up a white towel, put it into his left hand and said, "OK, I'm going to help you to experience hypnosis, but first I want to test out your so-called 'control.'" I began by positioning his left arm straight out to the side of his body, horizontal to the floor. I said to him, "Now, your job is to hold that towel as tightly as you can. When you don't expect it, I'm going to pull it away from you. I may walk behind you and then sneak up, or I may just grab it from you." His arm stiffened and he had a "death grip" on the towel as he said, "No you won't!" At this point I made several moves as if to try and grab the towel. As I did so, his intense concentration on the towel and me increased. After a few more "attempts," I stepped behind him and said, "Get ready, I'm going to stand where you can't see me and when you least expect it, I'm going to jump out and get it."

At this point his left arm had been cataleptic for several minutes. To an observer trained in hypnotic phenomena, it would have been apparent that he was in "that state." However, he had not yet experienced his "proof." I reached over toward his left hand, slowly with my left hand.

At the same time, I reached toward his right arm with my right hand and rested it gently on his right forearm. I then slowly lifted his right arm up, off the arm of the chair. I held his arm up, very still, for several seconds, and then I let go. His right arm remained up, without moving, and he continued to stare at the towel in his left hand.

I had planned on going no further, but the group instructor had a different goal in mind. Without my knowledge, he had taken a sterile needle from a drawer. While I was continuing to make gestures at the towel "as if" I was going to grab it, the instructor inserted the needle in the subject's right hand. This was done in the fleshy part, between the thumb and first finger. (When I saw what he had done, I was so surprised that I think I went into "that state" myself.) The subject didn't move a muscle, nor acknowledge what had happened. He gave every indication of being totally unaware of "his condition." We, the attendees and instructors, all stood observing the subject while he continued to stare at the towel, without movement or comment.

After three or four minutes, he looked up and said, "Well, nothing is happening. When are you going to begin?" Everyone began laughing at that statement, and he said, "What the hell is so funny?" He then began looking around at the group. He suddenly spotted the needle in his hand and exclaimed, "When the hell did that happen? I didn't even feel it!"

EXAMPLE 3: DISCUSSION

By his initial comments, the subject had indicated that not only was control a major issue for him, but that he was *proud* of his "control." Utilization simply required giving him something to control—the towel—and then "helping" him to worry about his control (my threat to take the towel away). As has already been stated, people often enter their own hypnotic state to avoid someone else's. Based on that, I could be sure he would enter into hypnosis to avoid my "control." It was also a good bet that, as long as I didn't point that fact out to him, he would cooperate by "controlling" everything. As for his developing spontaneous analgesia, that is not an uncommon occurrence: that is, many individuals spontaneously develop partial or complete analgesia when entering a hypnotic state. (Erickson, M. and Rossi, E., 1979; Kroeger, 1963).

EXAMPLE 4:

I was asked to give a lecture/demonstration on the subject of utilization as a method of hypnotic induction. During a question and answer period, I was asked to give an example of utilization with the type of individual who fears "loss of control." I began to tell the group about the incident cited in Example 3 above. As I explained what had happened, I held my right arm out from my side, horizontally to the floor, as if I was holding the towel. I was, in effect, "showing" the group what had transpired.

As I continued, I noticed something interesting happening to a man in the front row. He was staring intently at my right hand, without blinking and without body movement. I continued to explain what had happened, and at the same time, I walked down off the stage, keeping my right arm fixed in its position. I walked slowly toward the man and said to him, "And what color is the towel you...SEE NOW." He replied, "White... It's a white dish towel." I said, "That's right! Now...I want you to hold it for me." With that he reached out and I put the "towel" into his left hand. I then gently extended his left arm straight out in front of his body. I then said, "As you close your eyes, I want you to continue to see the towel [his eyes closed], and then continue to go where you need...NOW...to go to remember something pleasant and useful to you...NOW."

The man's arm stayed cataleptic, and he sat, eyes closed, without movement, for almost ten minutes. During this period of time, I continued with my explanation as to what had happened at the dental meeting (example 3 above). The man slowly opened his eyes, lowered his arm and said, "You hypnotized me! I can't believe it, but I know it happened."

After the meeting was over, the man approached me. He asked if he could make an appointment to see me at my office. Before I could respond, a very elderly gentleman interrupted, and said, "If I hadn't been here to see it, I wouldn't believe it! Joe [not his real name] has been to dozens of hypnotists over the last ten years, and no one has been able to hypnotize him!" "You're kidding," I replied. "I didn't have to do anything. He did it to himself. Maybe if I had known how impossible he was, I could have failed, too."

Joe then ticked off an impressive list of well-known hypnotists who had "failed" with him. I replied, "Do you mean to say that you have been successful at failing to go where they wanted you to go, and instead you've gone where you wanted?" He nodded his head vigorously and said, "Yes... I mean no... Well, I guess so." I smiled and said, "You must be an Indian Scout, are you not?" He stared at me and said, "What's that supposed to mean?" I replied, "You seem very proud of all the scalps you've collected!"

EXAMPLE 4: DISCUSSION

I can only make some educated guesses as to why so many fine, well-known hypnotists had "failed" with Joe. In the first place, I don't think that they did fail. Joe was a "natural" hypnotic subject. However, he was also the type of individual who has set ideas as to how everything should be done. (This was later proved to be the case when we met at my office.) Therefore, it was a good bet that Joe would enter into hypnosis in his own unique way, and that he would resent direct orders or suggestions.

Secondly, Joe was what I term a "visual's visual"—that is, he hallucinates beautifully with his eyes wide open. In effect, he stares straight ahead and makes "movies." Since most traditional hypnotic inductions attempt to "cause" or "force" eye closure, Joe would probably respond by staring straight ahead. Once Joe was helped to make a "movie," he almost automatically went into the hypnotic state. During the lecture, Joe "saw" the towel and made his personal "movie" about it. By asking what color the towel was, I was, in effect, accepting his way of responding instead of trying to get him to do it my way. By asking him to hold the towel, I was taking his "movie" and redirecting it toward a goal. In this case, the goal was to produce a formal altered state. Since he visualized so well, it was a good bet that he would more or less "disconnect" from his kinesthetic experiences. Therefore, he wouldn't know where I put his arm, which made it easy to produce catalepsy.

EXAMPLE 5:

This example is really a consolidation of several individuals who come under the heading of "oppositional" or "paradoxical." Individuals in this category not only tend to do and respond exactly opposite of what you intend, but they often tend to drive therapists in general "A LITTLE CRAZY!"

The patient's complaints included not getting along with people in general, and anger at being told what to do. The patient had "tried" to be hypnotized, but would not "allow myself to respond."

ME: I believe that your skill of deciding for yourself is useful. The problem as I see it is that you have lost the ability to be flexible, or to have choice as to when to be stubborn.

PT: Are you saying that being stubborn is not bad, and that I don't have to get rid of it?

ME: That's right. However, a patient once told me that being grown up includes the ability to do what is in your best interest even if someone else suggests it!

PT: I don't agree. I...

ME: [Interrupting] That's good. I'm glad you don't agree. Now I would like you to continue helping me by refusing to do what I tell you.

PT: Do you mean that you want me to fight you?

ME: Yes! You will be very helpful to me by continuing not to cooperate.

PT: OK. That's easy!

ME: Wait a minute. You just agreed with me. That's not fair. That's cooperating.

PT: What? I'm confused.

ME: Good. Now you've got it. Keep on doing it just that way. Now I don't want you to raise your left arm.

PT: [Slowly raises left arm while beginning to look confused.]

ME: Don't keep your arm just like that.

PT: [Arm stays straight out, stiff.]

ME: That's fine. Now I want your right arm to get very light.

PT: [Right arm noticeably presses down.]

ME: Thank you. You're really doing a good job of helping by not helping.

PT: [Begins to have a "glazed" look.] I'm really getting confused.
            I'm not sure what to do next.

ME: Well...lower your left arm.

PT: [Responds by lowering his left arm.]

ME: No! No! Now you're cooperating by doing what I'm asking. I
            want you to cooperate by not doing what I ask.

PT: My head is spinning. I'm not sure what to do next.

ME: Well, don't go into hypnosis...*NOW*...Keep on staring at me
            instead!

PT: What? [Stares a moment, eyes close, and a look of relief crosses
            his face.]

ME: Now, stop relaxing so deeply so quickly.

PT: [Stiffens, then noticeably relaxes.]

ME: Whatever you do, only drift as deeply as you decide...*NOW*...
            and don't let that arm get light and float up [not specifying
            which arm, so that he can both resist and comply].

EXAMPLE 5: DISCUSSION

I believe that the above example is self-explanatory. Using the
patient's oppositional nature, I structured a double bind (or maybe
several): The patient could cooperate by not doing what I asked, or
cooperate by doing what I asked. It didn't matter which method he chose.
My experience has been that, after two or three sessions of the above
craziness, the patient stops being oppositional in therapy. More
importantly, they stop being oppositional in the real world.

EXAMPLE 6:

The following occurred during an in-house training seminar for
medical doctors at a local hospital. After demonstrating several rapid
induction methods and utilization techniques, I asked the group to
practice with each other. While most of the group was doing that, one
young doctor approached me and said, "I'd really like to be able to
experience hypnosis, but for me it's impossible." I asked him if he would

allow me to use him as a subject when the group had finished their practice. He agreed to do so. When the group had finished their practice session, I asked Dr. "S" to come up and take a seat. I then explained to the group that Dr. "S" believed that it was impossible for him to go into the hypnotic state; that since that was what he believed, I must accept that as true for him. I then pointed out that as doctors, they did not have to *undergo* surgery to learn to *perform* surgery, nor did they have to get a disease in order to diagnose it. I turned to Dr. "S" and said, "Would you agree with what I just said?" He nodded his head and said, "Yes, that makes sense."

ME: Now, you are here to learn something about hypnosis, and so are your colleagues, is that correct? [His head nods "yes."] Since you don't need to have surgery to learn to perform surgery, it stands to reason that you don't have to be hypnotized to learn how to produce the hypnotic state.

"S": Yes, that makes sense also.

ME: Good, we agree. Now I'm going to ask you to simply pretend that you are a great hypnotic subject. That will allow your colleagues to learn a great deal, and of course, so will you. Is that OK?

"S": [Dr. "S" nods his head] Sure, I'd like to be of some help.

ME: Now, pretending that you're a good subject, what would your body position be if you were in hypnosis?

"S": I guess relaxed and loose.

ME: Relaxed and loose ...good ...can you show me what that would look like?

"S": [Rearranges his body position into what looks like a relaxed position.]

ME: How would your head be ...straight up like it is now, or kind of down toward your chest?

"S": I guess it would be down a little...like this [lowers his head].

ME: Eyes opened or closed...NOW?

"S":   Closed. [closes his eyes]

ME: Good! Now pretending that you are going into a deep hypnotic
          state, I would like you to experience, within yourself, what you
          would experience. Later you can tell us about it.

"S":   [Nods head slowly, breathing begins to noticeably slow]

ME: [Supposedly to the audience, but really directed toward Dr. "S"]
          Now, if he were really in hypnosis, I would ask him to take his
          time in discovering...NOW...where he learned to believe that
          he had to hold onto certain limitations, and to discover from his
          creative self what he needs to have at least three new choices
          [Pause for 3 or 4 minutes.] I would also ask him to continue to
          learn and ignore us, and to not return here until his unconscious
          mind was satisfied as to his new choices.

At this point in time, Dr. "S" appears to be "long gone" and is
evidencing all the classical manifestations of trance: slow, deep
breathing; immobility; total physical relaxation; and no responses to the
noises or questions from the audience. Dr. "S" continued to "pretend" to
be in hypnosis while I held a question and answer session. This went on
for ten minutes while we all watched Dr. "S."

I then said, "He can continue as long as he wants and as long as is
necessary, or whichever comes first." I spent another 15 minutes
answering questions, and then the meeting was adjourned. There was just
one small problem. Dr. "S" was continuing to "pretend" that he was in
that state. Several of the doctors came up and began to watch Dr. "S"
while he sat "pretending." One of the doctors said, "When will he come
out of it?" I replied, "Normally, you would let him continue as deeply
and as long as he needs to continue. However, since everyone is waiting
to leave, you could say to him that he can continue learning after he
returns here, and he will return here when he realizes *now* how full his
bladder is." Within two minutes, Dr. "S" began moving in the chair, and
then his eyes opened. He said, "What happened? Where is everyone?
I've got to go to the bathroom in the worst way."

EXAMPLE 6: DISCUSSION

Since Dr. "S" had signed up for the program, he was, in all probability, there to learn. On the other hand, he "believed" that being hypnotized

was impossible for him. The task, therefore, was to find a way to utilize those two factors in some manner that was acceptable to him. "Accepting" that his being hypnotized was impossible, by stating that to the group, utilized *that* aspect. Emphasizing the learning aspects of the meeting, and then asking him to "pretend" for the purpose of learning, utilized *that* part. By structuring the situation so he could merely "pretend," allowed him to believe it was still "impossible" and yet he could still learn by simulation. Of course, if you pretend to raise your right hand, you will, in most cases, actually raise it.

EXAMPLE 6: COMMENTS AND FOLLOW-UP

Asking a subject or patient to pretend is, in itself, a powerful utilization technique. Pretending elicits memories of those aspects necessary to "pretend." I have asked individuals to pretend that they know what it would take to solve some specific problem, or to overcome a fear, etc. In the vast majority of cases, their pretended answers are important keys that unlock the right doors. In addition, the "pretend" approach is a powerful induction technique. When a subject tells you what he would experience if he were "really" in hypnosis, he has, in most cases, given you the exact map to follow. Last, but not least, Dr. "S," as a result of his "pretend" hypnotic experiences, began to experience changes in some important areas of his life.

Several weeks after his experience, he took me to lunch. He told me that he and his wife had been having some difficulties, and that he had not been able to "get it on" sexually with his wife in almost a year. His wife had been claiming that he was almost always uptight, and that he seldom "let go." He said that since the training class, he had begun to loosen up, and was finding it easier to "let things happen," and that he was becoming sexually active with his wife. In addition, he informed me that for one week following the class, he had a tendency to "sort of drift away and lose track of everything, whenever I'm alone with nothing important to do." I told him that he was an excellent hypnotherapist, and that his ability to not understand was helping him to gain understanding.

EXAMPLE 7:

"B," a 38-year-old doctor, was referred to me with a "list" of presenting problems. He had made out the list very carefully. He informed me that his list was in the order of the problems' importance. "B" told me that he had taken several courses in "professional" hypnosis

(I assume that other courses were to him "unprofessional" courses), and that he attended many hypnosis workshops. He also stated that he often used self-hypnosis, but had been unable to solve his problems with that approach. Additionally, "B" had been in psychotherapy for nearly a year, and he claimed that he had made little or no progress. I asked him why he continued for a year when it wasn't, according to him, doing much good. He replied, "I like to finish what I start, and I'm a very patient man." When asked what he did for relaxation, he answered, "When I want to relax, I more or less drop out. I accomplish that by turning on some music at a very low volume. I then close my eyes and really make myself tune in to the music. I then start a process of drifting." (I wonder if you, the reader, have figured out what his preferred conscious system is?)

After gathering some additional information, I began to tell him several metaphors. The thrust of these metaphors was to "remind" him that we do many things without thinking about them in specific, step-by-step detail. I wanted him to remember that there are many areas in which we rely on our unconscious processes; that this frees our "logical" mind for other matters. (I'm sure that the reader can "see" that "B" was a very logical person: problems in a list, systematically studying hypnosis, etc. You can...NOW RECOGNIZE...that his preferred system is auditory.)

As I would tell him a metaphor, I would lean slightly to my right, and talk softly in a monotone (remember the music). When giving him so-called "factual, logical" information, I would lean to my left, and talk more rapidly and with tonal animation. After a short time, when I would lean right and switch to a monotone, "B" would sit perfectly still and stare intently. When I leaned to my left, he would "fidget" and his face was animated. Toward the end of our first session, "B" said, "I know you're doing something to me. I can feel it happening, but I can't figure it out. Aren't you going to try and hypnotize me?" I laughed and said, "I'm still trying to figure out how to get you to stop going into hypnosis so well!"

EXAMPLE 7: SESSION 2

Our second meeting was basically a repetition of our first session. The metaphors were now more directed toward his "list." Whenever I finished a metaphor, I would stare at him without blinking for several seconds. I would then blink several times, switch to my left and give him some "logical" information. As we neared the end of the session, he again said, "Aren't you going to try and hypnotize me?" I again laughed, leaned to my right, and just stared at him. "B" immediately "froze" and stared back. I then sat straight up, and "B" blinked several times and said, "Hey, have you been hypnotizing me all along?" "That would be telling," I replied, while I nodded my head slowly "yes." "Besides, there's no such thing as hypnosis."

I then leaned to my right, and moved my lips as if I was speaking. However, I wasn't making a sound. "B" "froze" again, his eyes glazed, and his body began to slump. Very softly I said, "Not yet. Next week will be soon enough." I then sat straight up in my chair. "B" blinked several times and then said, "Wow. That was strange. I know you hypnotized me, but I don't know how." With that we ended our second session.

EXAMPLE 7: SESSION 3

"B" entered my office and sat down with an expectant look on his face. (You could say he was altering his state in preparation of having his state altered.) I asked him if anything surprising had occurred during the last week. He replied, "Yes, quite a bit. I have been laughing more and I seem to be looser in the way I move. My staff has commented about how much calmer I seem to be. The only problem is, I can't figure out why."

I responded by telling him, "Good. You are a very logical person, but in the past you've been totally illogical in your attempts to solve your problems. After all, if logic were the answer, you would have logically solved the problems. Since logic has failed you, it's illogical to do more of the same." (As I was giving him that logical, illogical explanation, I slowly shifted to my right and also shifted to monotone.)

I reached for his left hand, and slowly and gently lifted it up. When his hand and arm were about one foot off the arm of the chair, I held his hand still. I said to him (still in a monotone), "Now you know where your hand is because you can see it. However, even though you're a doctor, you would have difficulty naming all the muscles, in the exact logical order, that are...*keeping your hand and arm exactly as it is.*" (Unconscious suggestion for arm catalepsy.) At this point, "B" was completely still, was staring without blinking, and was totally En-Tranced with what was transpiring.

I continued: "Now...as you close your eyes, you won't be able to know where your hand is by seeing it. Instead, you can be very successful by allowing yourself to experience all of the feelings of it." (Much of what is now being said is directed toward two goals: 1) trance induction; and 2) metaphoric approach to his "real" problem—being shut off as to experiencing feelings in general.) "And, as you continue to connect to all those good feelings, without action...and perhaps without understanding, then my voice will continue to be as if soft music, and you can continue to drift."

At this point, "B" was given some direction toward the resolution of his problems and then told, "Your arm will probably remain stuck, just as you have been, until you discover how to become even more flexible in your personal life." Twenty minutes later, "B's" arm moved slowly down. Instead of terminating his hypnotic state, he appeared to be deepening it. I told him that his unconscious mind would decide if he was ready to return to "this time and place," or to continue with what he was doing if that was more important. "B" stayed in "that state" for another hour and fifteen minutes. I had to use one of our other offices to see my next appointments.

Over the next several weeks, the changes in "B" were not only dramatic, but delightful to watch. He put it best when he said, "Everything used to seem so serious and important, life or death. Now, I'm having some fun with my life, and saving my serious side for truly serious problems. The funny thing is that I'm accomplishing more with less effort."

EXAMPLE 7: DISCUSSION

The above example is filled with utilization. Often the induction processes and therapeutic goal processes were completely intertwined. That makes it somewhat difficult to make a clear delineation between the two. Certain factors, however, can be separated and spotlighted.

"B" had been trained in traditional hypnotic techniques, and had been practicing them on himself. However, "it" wasn't working. Therefore, any use of so-called traditional approaches would no doubt meet the same fate. In other words, any overt attempt to hypnotize "B" would probably not succeed. He gave support to that interpretation when, at the end of the first session, he said, "Aren't you going to *try* to hypnotize me." (In this context, the word "try" implies: I know it won't be successful, but let's try.)

In addition, "B" had been in formal psychotherapy for almost a year, with little or no acknowledged results. Helping him to gain more "insight" or "logical" understanding would produce a lot more of the same...*NOTHING*.

"B" had given me the information needed to help him experience an altered state. This information was conveyed when he explained what happened when he listened to music on low volume. By leaning right and talking in a slow monotone, I hoped to accomplish two things: The leaning right would itself become an unconscious suggestion to enter into hypnosis; the monotone would recreate his experience of hearing something in the background while he "drifted." His responses to these tactics indicated that they would "do the trick."

He had also told me that he was a patient man. Telling him long, drawn-out metaphors would insure he would have plenty to be patient about: Listening to me, trying to understand my point, waiting for me to "try" to hypnotize him, while drifting due to my monotone. Last, but perhaps most important: pointing out to him that he would have to *feel*...his arm in order to remember where it was, required him to get in touch (or pay attention, or tune in) to his internal (kinesthetic) sensations, while, at the same time, he was attempting to listen to my monotone metaphors. The combination of his "patience," "drifting when listening to something soft and low," and my pseudo-logic all combined to utilize his skills and experiences to help him move...NOW...to new experiences.

I could no doubt "DO" one hundred pages on utilization. I don't want to use a sledge hammer to drive a thumb tack. While what you have read about utilization was directed primarily toward producing the hypnotic state, utilization is even more useful as a therapeutic strategy. It is beyond the scope and intent of this work to outline utilization in detail as a therapeutic approach. However, throughout this work, I have attempted to "sneak" in examples of several utilization methods.

CREATIVE UTILIZATION

For those of you who wish to take a creative leap, the following hints may be useful for you to utilize: Utilize the compulsive personality's compulsiveness to compulsively carry out assignments that lead to new behaviors, which break up the compulsiveness; utilize the rigid person's need to be right, to have them carry out the assignment of being wrong, just right, and to enter into hypnosis in the "right" way; utilize the phobic's ability to generate feelings (Kinesthetic) from their internal pictures (Visual) to generate new feelings from new internal pictures; utilize the depressive's "skill" of holding on to feelings (depression) no matter what any one says or does, to learn to hold on to *good* feelings in spite of the ups and downs of life.

In summary, you can...*BEGIN NOW*...to look at the presenting problems as a form of unique skill. Once you do that, your task is to discover the method behind that skill, and then to redirect it. The grand master of this form of utilization was the incomparable Milton Erickson, M.D. He utilized his own physical limitations as hypnotic induction cues. He utilized the patient's personality, history, traits and problems as techniques for change. Many wise and well-versed individuals have written about the techniques of Dr. Erickson. These individuals all tend to have a different "answer" as to what his work was based on. Whatever the truth may be, I believe that if you approach Dr. Erickson's work looking for consistent utilization, you will be consistently rewarded,

In some situations (I'm sure that Dr. Erickson would have agreed), you need not do anything to produce hypnosis via utilization. Several years ago, a friend of mine got married. He asked me to a small dinner party to meet his new wife. He told me she was excited about the prospect of meeting a "real" hypnotist. He informed me that she was afraid that if she looked at my eyes she would get "put under." When I arrived for the dinner party, my friend greeted me at the door. He led me in to meet his wife. As he introduced me, she reached out to shake my hand, and then her eyes caught mine. She began to stare, and then...*BAM!* Her eyes closed, she slumped and I had to reach out and catch her. You could say that my presence, combined with her belief system and expectations, produced an interesting phenomenon... You could say that she had hypnotized herself into being hypnotized by my eyes. But, of course, and lest we forget, there's no such thing as...

XV

Weighing Anchors

RED LIGHT DISTRICT

If you were driving down a busy uptown street, and suddenly a green light turned red, would you...*stop now!* It's probably safe for me to assume that you would, under most circumstances. If we were to examine this simple act of stopping, we could then move forward into a new area together. We might discover some complex and interesting "things." We might agree that the red light has become a simple symbol that elicits a complex sequence of behavior which we would call "stopping." Within the behavior called "stopping" are included perceptual problem-solving skills, psycho-motor, neuro-motor activity—eye, hand, foot, etc.—coordination, driving skills and much more, all chained together as a complex sequence called "stopping for a red light."

The red light, through learning processes, has become what behaviorists term an "external stimulus." Other theorists would call the red light an "anchor" or "trigger" (Bandler and Grinder). They would claim, and I would agree, that the red light now *anchors*: that is, it has associated with it a whole series of behaviors through a more or less coded, sequential and repetitive manner. We might even say that the anchor (red light) is so strong that even if you are not the driver, certain aspects of the response are elicited anyway. (How many times have you jammed on the non-existent brake when you were the passenger and not the driver?)

ANCHORS: A SIMPLISTIC DEFINITION

Anchors can be most easily understood if we reduce them to a simple stimulus-response construct. But no one promised you that this book was to be easy. Accepting the easy definition will help you to not learn the subtleties of anchors. For those of you who want it easy, here goes: Anchors (triggers) = any stimulus that triggers a set of internal responses and/or actions.

However, you might want to consider everything within human experience is, in effect, an anchor, or, if you will, a red light that sets into motion a chain of responses. Take the words you are now reading, comfortably deep or deeply comfortable. Each word is an anchor for an experience of understanding. As you read each word, those symbols or anchors lead you to an unconscious process that includes, but is not limited to, interpreting the word itself and attaching your personal experience and understanding to it.

For example, as you read the word "house," what memories will that evoke in you...NOW? Try an experiment, if you will. Get together with several friends, and give each one a paper and pencil (or pen or crayon). Say the word "house," and ask each to write down in detail what s/he is reminded of. The diversity of triggered or anchored memories should be very interesting, for someone.

In most cases, the word "cumquat" will not evoke the same anchored response as the word "sex" will now! Anchors, like all other experiences (which themselves are anchors), come in different intensities and are different for each one of us. What turns me on may turn you off, and if what turns you on turns me off...well... However, words are only *one* form of anchors. Again, everything can be, and is, for someone at some time an anchor. If, for our purposes, we were to understand anchors to be any trigger—internal or external—which evokes within someone a certain set response in all or most all cases, regardless of whether we label the response good or bad, and when such response is ritualized, we should have an anchor for the word anchor.

ANCHORS IN POST-HYPNOTIC RESPONSE

If we were to get a little metaphysical, we might say that anchors are a form of post-hypnotic suggestion. That is, that circumstances, situations, people, schools, smells, traumas, etc., have suggested certain responses to all the anchors in our world. (Remember, if you've now forgotten, there's no such thing as hypnosis.) Within the framework of traditional hypnosis, the hypnotist might "suggest" that at a snap of the fingers, the subject will remember his/her 5th birthday. If this suggestion were successful, we could say that the snap of the fingers had become the anchor to trigger the suggested memory.

Now, I am going to upset some of you who might believe that the concept of anchoring is new. Boy, have you been anchored if you believe that! If, for the moment, we leave aside natural anchors (whatever they are), and limit this part of our discussion to anchors and hypnosis, we could together learn something new. Modern old-time hypnotists were the first to discover "suggested" internal anchors (unless specified to not be the case, from now on we will discuss anchors as suggested intentional phenomena). Old-fashioned trance induction was and is a very long, tedious procedure. The modern old-time hypnotist discovered what are now called "reinduction cues." Before the subject was "counted out" (or whatever) from hypnosis, the following type of suggestion would be given: "...when I touch your forehead [shoulder, what have you] and count [backward, forward, up, down, it doesn't matter], you will re-enter into this pleasant [deep, comfortable] state." (Kroeger, 1963; Wolberg, 1964).

Where this post-hypnotic suggestion "took" you would have, in effect, a one-trial learning anchor. From that point on, each time the hypnotist triggered that anchor, the subject would re-enter the so-called trance state. In some cases, any other person triggering the anchor would find the subject entering into a trance. Pavlov, with his development of classical stimulus-response conditioning, was one of the first to recognize anchors and to realize that anything could be used as a stimulus to produce a response. He discovered, in his work with dogs, that food—the unconditioned stimulus (US)—leads to an unconditioned response (UR): salivating. Pair a bell to the US, and in a short while, the bell becomes a conditioned stimulus that elicits the UR. Another way of describing that condition would be: The bell has become an anchor (trigger) that produces the response of salivating, as if the bell were food.

Andrew Salter *(Conditioned Reflex Therapy,* 1961) held that hypnosis—that is, the *state* of hypnosis as separate from the method of producing hypnosis—is, itself, a series of conditioned responses. He further concluded that all symptoms, regardless of the labels, are a result of conditioned inhibitions, and that all humans are born with the capacity to be outgoing, spontaneous and fun-loving. (We might say born utilizing fully the right hemisphere, as well as the left.) Thus, we are conditioned in painful association (anchors) to be afraid of our natural state and instead to become inhibited. (Perhaps to become too left-hemispheric; see Chapter X, "Left Meets Right Meets Left.")

Whether Salter's theory is correct or not does not take away from the implied conclusion: Individuals have the ability to associate unrelated (in reality) stimuli to produce complex responses. We might choose to call the stimulus an "anchor" which produces a set of learned responses.

Let's suppose little Johnnie is trying independence on for size. He pulls himself up to his full (fill in average height of a five-year-old) and thus, towering under his father, he says, "NO! I won't!" Father becomes enraged and jumps to his feet pointing at Johnnie and yells, "Don't you say 'no' to me or I'll knock your block off. Get to your room." Several years later, Johnnie is sitting in a therapist's office claiming that he can't say "no" to anyone he *sees as being in authority over him*. If you were to conclude that, for Johnnie, saying the word "no" has become an anchor that elicits great fear, then you are right.

What you have read this far has anchored you into an understanding. In my clinical practice, I have heard people claim that certain facial expressions, tones of voice, gestures, postures, words, smells, etc. have caused them to: get depressed, get anxious, throw up, get headaches, go crazy, etc., etc. You could consider all of the above conditioned reflex responses or anchors.

You've probably remembered by now that Pavlov conditioned a dog to salivate at the sound of a bell. Wrong! The dog conditioned a bunch of scientists to ring a bell whenever the dog salivated. Be careful to determine now who is anchoring whom.

ERICKSON AND ANCHORS

Milton Erickson discovered some very powerful uses for anchors which have influenced several individuals, including myself, in our interest, understanding and uses of anchors. Erickson observed that if he asked a patient to sit just as he had the last time he experienced trance, and Erickson began talking in the same manner and/or about the same subject as the last trance experience, the patient would re-enter the trance state without any so-called induction. Erickson named this technique "recapitulation."

A colleague of mine, David Dobson, and I became fascinated with this phenomenon, and began experimenting with it. In our experiments (separately and then comparing notes), we discovered (or stumbled upon) a very interesting additional phenomenon: If you could get a subject to remember a specific situation in his imagination, he would often manifest all the emotional responses that the subject associated with the actual incident *as if he were actually there.*

In one instance, a woman complained that when her husband touched her in a sexual way, she became "sick to my stomach. I feel like throwing up." I asked her to close her eyes and remember being with her husband, hearing his voice, smelling his after-shave, feeling his touch. At this point, she opened her eyes and began gagging. This was another form of recapitulation without a formal trance or regression and yet...

Dr. Dobson and I both concurred that the individuals were entering trance and regressing spontaneously whenever they were asked to "imagine a situation" and all their systems were involved (Kinesthetic, Visual, Auditory, and in some cases, Gustatory and Olfactory). Our experiments and observations led us to conclude that individuals were suffering the pain they suffered as a result of more or less powerful anchors which acted as if they were hypnotic suggestions, and produced powerful, repetitive conditional responses—just as a red light triggers a complex series of actions leading to stopping.

SPONTANEOUS ANCHORS

Many years ago, a serendipitous event brought out the ease with which people are anchored, the importance of anchors, and how anchors could not only be *anything,* but could produce responses entirely unrelated to the anchor itself. I had put a man into hypnosis while he was sitting in my office recliner (actually he put himself there), and asked him to go back to the source of a particular problem he was having. All hell broke loose. He cried, moaned, twisted around, and more. When I asked him to signal if he wanted to end this trance, he signaled "no." He carried on this way for about 20 minutes, and then terminated his hypnotic state, claiming he had learned a great deal. He returned the following week for his next appointment, and I greeted him in the reception area. He looked relaxed and was smiling, and said he had had a great week with substantial reduction of his symptoms (one of which was asthma).

We walked into my office, and he sat down in the recliner... *BANG!*...the picture of Dorian Gray. His smile slipped away, his tone changed, he began to wheeze, cry, moan, etc. I asked him what was wrong. He said he didn't know, and I was very puzzled by his response. Then I noticed his eyes were dilated and he appeared to be "out of it" or in "that state." I took his hand and pulled him out of the recliner, and said sharply, "Look at me now and recall a time you were happy about something you just did." Slowly, his breathing changed, his face relaxed, the wheezing stopped, and he began to smile. I asked him to sit in another chair, which he did without any problem. After obtaining his permission for him to "experience" something, I asked him to again sit in the recliner. As he approached it, his body, posture and facial expression began to change, and as he sat down, all the previous behavior began to re-emerge. He jumped out of the chair and said he wasn't going to sit there "cause the chair is doing something to me." He was right. The chair had become an anchor, or post-hypnotic re-induction, that led him to re-experience his last painful time in that chair, with all the attendant memory and emotional response which he now blamed the chair for.

PAVLOV AND ANCHORS

The above incident made several things clear to me. The chair had become a conditioned stimulus—like Pavlov's bell—in one trial; and a person could spend years in therapy trying to find out why they had a phobia about a chair. If a chair could become such a powerful anchor, so too could a word, a tone, a touch—or whatever. The anchor need not have any logical relationship to the response the anchor produces. (Just recently, I "helped" an individual to develop a mini-phobic response to a telephone, and then used the same telephone to elicit memories and responses relating to the first time he had fallen in love.)

This incident also caused a regression (in me) to a time three years earlier. A professor of neurological psychology and I had a "little" disagreement during a lecture he was giving on classical conditioning and neurological responses. I asked him a theoretical question: "If an individual could be conditioned to respond in a certain way to a given stimulus, could you use the same stimulus and/or response to trigger a new and different response? For example, if a doorbell triggered anxiety, could you help the individual to either 1) respond in a different way to the doorbell itself so that the doorbell became a trigger for say, relaxation, or 2) help the individual to use the first subjective feelings of anxiety—i.e., tightness—to trigger a response such as relaxation?"

The professor thought for a while, did some mathematical formulas on the blackboard, and then stated, "Theoretically it's possible, particularly with animals, but probably unrealistic when it comes to people because of all the uncontrollable variables." He asked me what methodology I would use and what apparatus did I believe would be needed to experiment with. I responded that I wasn't sure of the methodology, but the so-called "apparatus" would be hypnosis. He almost choked as he said, "Hypnosis!? It doesn't exist, and even if I could get people to respond as I had suggested, it wouldn't matter since hypnosis wasn't science but witchcraft." In retrospect, I can "see" that he had been hypnotized into believing hypnosis didn't exist, and that the word "hypnosis" was the post-hypnotic "cue" (anchor) that elicited his somewhat weird response. Nonetheless, the incident with the recliner triggered the memory of my earlier question or theory, and I again began to wonder if it could be done. Based on what had happened to the man and his response to the recliner, I knew it was more than possible; that it happened all the time in all of our lives.

CALM CONDITIONING

My first effort, or experiments, with what would later be termed "anchors," and the methods that would become part of what I call Unconscious Restructuring®, were very primitive. I called it "Calm Conditioning." Simply put, I would ask an individual to "remember" the last time they were, for example, afraid. As they "remembered," I would observe them for signs of discomfort such as tightness in the body or in the face; or rapid breathing; or?

When it looked to me that they were "remembering" it by feeling it, I would touch them (usually on the arm) and say, "Good. Hold on to that feeling so that you can become very familiar with how it feels inside." Next, I would ask them to go back and re-experience that feeling again, but in slow motion, to become aware of the first strong physical sensation such as tightening in the stomach or chest, or wherever, and to signal me by lifting the first finger of their right hand when they had that sensation. I would then touch them on the spot I had touched before and tell them to begin.

When they signaled I would then apply a little more pressure to my touch for a few moments, and then remove my hand. Then, I would ask them to take several deep breaths and think of the beach or mountains or anything pleasant. The next step was to ask them to remember the most pleasant, relaxing place they have ever been—or to make one up in their imagination—and to signal when they had accomplished that. They were then asked to see themselves in that place again until they felt the calm, relaxed feelings that went with that experience, and to think of a word or two as a code to remind them of that pleasant place. I would then have them "practice" saying the code word and seeing that place and feeling those relaxed feelings.

At this point, when we were successful, the individual had an associated response to my touching them on the arm and asking them to remember the feeling of anxiety and another more pleasant associated response to their code word. (I had not yet figured out that this procedure could be accomplished without the need of code words.) The next step was to have them close their eyes and think of some situation that usually caused them to get anxious, and to signal when they had thought of it. At the same time, I would touch the spot on their arm to help them "remember" the anxious feeling they were to find. As soon as they signaled, I would stop touching them and say somewhat sharply, "Stop. [A pattern interruption.] Say your code word to yourself and see yourself there, feeling those pleasant feelings."

This procedure would be practiced many times (6 or 8) and then the individual, who by now would, in most cases, be in "that state" of hypnosis, would be instructed as follows: "Each time you feel that first signal of "anxiety" such as [filled in with what they had reported as the first signal], you are to think of your code word and see yourself there, feeling those comfortable feelings. As you practice this procedure, it will become more and more automatic until soon it will happen, in all the appropriate circumstances, without thinking and without your conscious awareness of having gone to your special place."

PROTOCOL PROCEDURE

In spite of the primitiveness of this first approach, and my lack of understanding of anchoring and systems (Visual—Kinesthetic—Auditory), it produced excellent results for the majority of people. Typically, they would report that when they used it, they would calm down; and many people reported that, within a few days, they were getting calm without thinking about it at all.

We might conclude that they were using a new anchor automatically which was generalizing to their real world. I would like to suggest that you...*NOW...consider doing this procedure* in a more updated form. Follow the above, but add the following refinements: Ask your client/patient to see the area that causes... (e.g., anxiety), and to see themselves looking tense until it looks "just right," and then to hear themselves as they sound when they are... (e.g., tense), and to signal you when they have accomplished that. When they signal, ask them to float into the picture and into those "uncomfortable feelings." When they signal they have done that and/or when you see evidence of their discomfort, touch them with light pressure on the arm (or ?) Then ask them to float out of the picture and out of the uncomfortable feelings and, as they are doing that, remove your hand; that is, stop touching them. Next, test your work.

Touch the spot and ask them to get back into that picture and observe if they again show signs of discomfort. If they do, you have "a take." If not, repeat until you get the desired results. Next, after you have ascertained their first signal—i.e., tight face—repeat the same procedure as the above for their calm, relaxed place, and add a touch in a *new* spot when they signal they have that comfort. (Again, ask them to see the place and then float into it, etc., and to think of a code word.) (Remember systems.)

With some people you may have to ask them to remember the feeling of…and then build a picture. However, make an effort to use seeing without feeling first. (The reason for that will be explained in the section on Therapeutic Applications in the next chapter, "Anchors Away.") Test this work: i.e., touch the new spot and ask them to think of the code word, and watch for signs you have a take. Now, use the rest of the procedure; that is, ask them to remember something that upsets them while touching the discomfort spot, and as soon as they signal or show signs, ask them to stop and say their code word and see themselves in their special place and float into etc., etc. As you tell them to stop, remove your touch from the "discomfort" spot and switch to touching their "comfort" spot. You may be pleasantly surprised at how well this procedure works and how many people enter "that state" without help.

I could be wrong. You may not be surprised as to how well it works and how many people *enter that state now! Now that you understand* the basics of anchors and the theory behind this, we together can move forward to *Anchors Away!*

XVI

Anchors Away

BASIC ANCHOR COLLAPSE

Several years ago, or once upon a time, I was asked to give a lecture and demonstration to a psychology class at California State University at Northridge. The professor, who was a very nice man, had told me beforehand that he did not believe in hypnosis, that it did not work anyway, but he felt his class should have the opportunity of hearing about it. I guess he wanted me to be the token hypnotist. To make matters even more interesting, he did not just introduce me and my subject, rather he was prepared with a long statement about his disbelief in hypnosis while stating he was open enough to give almost anybody a chance to speak about what they believe. It was as if he had told them I had designed the Titanic and was now going to prove that it had not sunk.

I decided that to survive my glowing introduction, I would have to demonstrate something dramatic, and on the professor. I knew from a previous conversation with him that he was going through a very painful divorce and was—according to him—fighting depression whenever, "I think about it." I thanked him for his introduction and, as he sat down on a long table at the front of the lecture hall, I walked over to him and ostensibly began talking to the class. I told them that I really appreciated the Professor's asking me here and introducing me, particularly at this time in his life when he was going through a very difficult period. His expression immediately began to change as he looked down to his right (kinesthetic), and evidenced discomfort.

At that point, I squeezed his right shoulder and said, "I know that's painful, isn't it?" He nodded slowly. I then removed my hand and said sharply, "How long will it take you *to remember now*...[said more slowly and with a lower tone: an embedded hypnotic suggestion to remember now] a time before you were 20 when you experienced something that felt so good that you knew everything was going to be exciting." (Taking a risk that most of us at some time before we were 20 did something or experienced something that was exciting.)

His head came up and his eyes began moving up to his left (visual recall), and his face began to relax. Slowly he smiled, and then blushed and said, very strongly, "I can remember." At this point, I had reached to his left shoulder and began to gently squeeze it. Without any explanation, I was making an effort to set up two anchors: touch on his right shoulder for the painful experience and touch on his left shoulder for the happy experience. Next I tested the work. I said to him, "That's a better feeling than the other, isn't it?" (Still squeezing his left shoulder.) He smiled and nodded vigorously. I then went on: "Much better than this uncomfortable feeling" (Here my voice became sad-sounding and my face looked sad, while I squeezed his right shoulder.)

The change was dramatic! He again looked as if his world was coming to an end: eyes down right, head lowered, lips quivering. I then switched to his left shoulder while saying, "You'd rather have these feelings, wouldn't you?" (Said with happy tone and smiling face.) He immediately looked up, took a deep breath, smiled and said: "What the hell are you doing to me?" I replied, "Confusion is new learning," and then I squeezed both shoulders *at the same time.*

His eyes glazed while he appeared to stare straight ahead, and he looked confused. I then instructed him as follows: "You can close your eyes and it will all *clear up comfortably"* (said slowly, in a low tone). He sat very still, breathing deeply for about three minutes, and then opened his eyes and asked what was going on. I reached over to squeeze his right shoulder to make sure the anchor was cancelled. He showed no response except, perhaps, a questioning one, but no "depression." I asked him to think about that painful situation, and to share with us what was different in his internal response. He turned his eyes up left (visual recall) and then down left (auditory) and then down right (kinesthetic) for one split second, and looked up at me and said, "It doesn't affect me like it did, and somehow I feel stronger and know it will be OK! What the hell did you do?"

I replied, "Nothing. There's no such thing as hypnosis so you must be hallucinating." (I guess what happened helped him to alter his belief system. He attended two of my seminars, Clinical Hypnosis: Innovative

Techniques®, and became a booster and utilizer of hypnosis and Unconscious Restructuring®.)

COLLAPSING ANCHORS: RATIONALE

Now, the above case may appear to be magic, and in a way it is. However, it is magic based on experimental research. In one classic experiment, experimental animals were conditioned to go to one side of a cage at the sound of a bell, and the other side at the sound of a buzzer. Almost like squeezing the left shoulder for one feeling and the right shoulder for another. When both stimuli were set off at the same time, the animals would appear to be confused and disoriented, and would then not respond to either stimuli. (Almost like what happened when I squeezed both of his shoulders at the same time...it does make you *wonder now* about the implications.)

Most individuals who are put through the above procedure report what comes very close to being cognitive dissonance; and some researchers claim that new learning does not take place *without* cognitive dissonance. Cognitive Dissonance has been defined as "a motivational state which exists when an individual's cognitive elements (attitudes, perceived behaviors, etc.) are inconsistent with each other." The tension produced by this state may be reduced by adding consonant elements, changing one of the dissonant element so that it is no longer inconsistent with the other, or "by reducing the importance of the dissonant elements." (Wolman, 1973, p. 66)

However, I want to caution you: as powerful as this technique can be, it isn't a panacea or a cure. All it does is to help an individual have "lowered emotionality" to a stressful situation, produce a calming effect and give the individual hope about solving their problem when they can experience such a marked change within several minutes. But, it's not a cure. It only accomplishes in five to ten minutes what three to eight traditional sessions might accomplish.

CASE 11: ANCHOR COLLAPSE

A brief case will underline this view: Patient was a 21-year-old man whose presenting problem was severe depression. In his own words: "My depression was so heavy that I think I made myself have a breakdown." He had spent three weeks in a hospital as a result of a voluntary commitment. After checking out of the hospital, he had entered therapy and, at the time of first seeing me, had been to five sessions of therapy.

He believed he was beginning to understand what had caused his depression, but he was still severely depressed.

He stated, "I'm beginning to lose hope. I'm in therapy and yet I'm still depressed almost all the time." While he described his depression verbally, he also "described" it physically: body posture slumped, eyes down right, voice sad and flat. As he talked about how "heavy" his depression was, and continued to evidence it physically, I reached over, gently touched his left knee, and said in a voice that mimicked his, "That's a heavy, awful feeling, isn't it?" He shook his head slowly. I then snapped my fingers (pattern interruption) and said, "Before your problem began, what did you really enjoy doing?" His head moved up slowly, he looked at me for a moment, and then his eyes went up left, and he said, "Baseball. I love the game! I'm a pitcher on the University team." I asked him if he ever had a really good day pitching. He smiled and said "Oh yeah! I once pitched a three hitter and struck out the last five batters in a row."

At this point, he had straightened up in the chair, and his voice was stronger and melodious. I replied, "You're kidding. Really?" He leaned forward, smiled, and said, "Yeah, honestly." At that moment, I reached over and gently touched his right knee and said, "That's great! I bet you really felt good!" He was now smiling and looked much better. To reinforce his plus (+) anchor, I asked him to describe how he felt inside after striking out the last five batters, and as he described the good feeling, I again touched his right knee. I repeated this procedure as he described, in response to my questions, how he looked and how he sounded. All of the above took less than ten minutes, and the young man was much more relaxed and he was smiling.

Next, I used the same procedure as on the professor described above. When he had "neutralized" out, I asked him to "Try Hard" (implying it would be very difficult) to remember the depressed feeling. He looked straight ahead for a few moments, then looked down right for a split second, brought his eyes back up level and said, "Hey, I'm having a hard time getting it back...anyhow I don't want it back. That's amazing. You mean there's hope for me after all?" As I nodded my head yes, I said, "What do you think?" He nodded his head and said, "Yeah, I'm going to beat it." He was referred back to his therapist who, several weeks later, reported that the young man was doing fine, was back in school and beginning to make some decisions about the situations that had led to his depression.

The above procedure is a basic "anchor collapse" and I will attempt to give you the skills to begin testing and practicing it so that you can judge the results for yourself. I want you to consider personal problems as an anchor or a series of anchors as explained in Chapter XIV, "Weighing Anchors." Your job is to help the individual have a choice as to their response to their painful anchors: that is, to collapse the undesired response or...*Anchors Away!*

ANCHOR COLLAPSE: BASIC PROCEDURE

If possible, you first want to establish a pleasant (+) anchor. While anchors can be set with visual, auditory and/or kinesthetic cues, I am going to recommend you begin with kinesthetic cues (physical touches) as they are the easiest to learn and use, even though beginning with kinesthetics might cause you to miss with a few individuals. However, if your client/patient is already in a bad place—e.g., depressed—don't work like mad to get them in a better place in order to set a + anchor and then throw them back into their bad place for the unpleasant (–) anchor. In that case, *start* by anchoring that feeling (– anchor).

I recommend that you sit directly in front of the individual, close enough to be able to touch their knees. Let's assume the individual's presenting complaint is being depressed whenever they are alone, but as they talk to you they appear to be pretty level. Ask them to remember a time they really felt good about something they accomplished while being alone; e.g. "Can you remember a time you took a ride by yourself and really enjoyed the scenery or a time you were working on your hobby and felt pleased." (Use your imagination.) When they say, "Yes," watch them carefully. Some people will begin to smile and show pleasure just from being asked. If they show a pleasurable response, gently, but firmly, press on one knee (doesn't matter which) and suggest, with a cheerful voice and a smile, something to the effect, "That's a nice feeling, isn't it?" (You are establishing the + anchor.)

If the individual merely says "yes," but doesn't evidence the "pleasure" in their expression, you must go further. (Systems become more important here; assume a visual person for this example.) Ask them to see that pleasurable situation, or to see how they looked in that pleasurable situation, or to "show me what you look like when you feel good." Next, ask them to remember the sounds of that experience, or how they sounded when they were feeling good. Next, ask them to describe what they feel when they feel good. As soon as they "show" the good feeling in their experience, establish the + anchor: that is, gently press on one knee (let's say the left) and say in a cheerful way, "That's a nice feeling," or "That feels good" or... Be creative but not incongruent. (At my training seminars, I have observed people saying, "That's a nice feeling, isn't it" while frowning and talking with a voice that would make an optimist sad.)

After you have established the + anchor, repeat the procedure to establish the – anchor; i.e., "Now, Mr. Smith, you told me you have been feeling depressed." Observe his facial expression, and, if it changes to one of sadness or depression, gently touch his other knee. If the facial expression doesn't change, use systems again: "How do you see yourself when you are depressed?" (Remember we are assuming a visual person for this example.) As soon as you observe the facial change, install the – anchor.

TESTING

At this point, in all probability, you will have established a + and a – anchor. You now want to test your work. This is either a simple procedure or a very easy one depending on your attitude: Touch the + anchor (left knee in our example) and, with a cheerful voice and face, say something like, "I'll bet you like this feeling better don't you?" Watch carefully to make sure that their general expression and demeanor matches the + anchor. If so, let go of the + anchor; touch the – anchor and say something like, "It's much better than the depressed feeling, isn't it?" (Be congruent; use a sad tone and facial expression.) Check to see that their expression, etc. matches the – anchor. If so, you have a take. (If not, go back and reinstall the + and – anchors, taking time to get the response you want.) After testing the – anchor, it is always a good choice to refire the + anchor; i.e., "Bet you really like this good feeling better," while touching the + anchor.

We can now stop and try to make rational sense out of what has just happened. If we do so, we have forgotten to remember there's no such thing as hypnosis. Another way to consider what you have accomplished is to assume that the touch on the left leg has become a hypnotic cue that helps the individual to respond to the "suggested" good feeling, while a touch on the right leg is a hypnotic (non-verbal) "suggestion" to respond with the "depressed" feeling.

Now that's crazy. How can we call that stuff hypnosis? No one was wearing a cape or waving a crystal ball, or telling the subject to go deeper and deeper. So, don't call it hypnosis. Call it anchoring, or stimulus response or magic. It doesn't matter because deep down, comfortably, you know what it really is. (Those of you who are experienced in so-called traditional hypnosis may notice some interesting phenomena. While inserting and testing + and – anchors, you will see many individuals evidencing pupil dilation, altered breathing rates, flaccidity of the facial muscles and an almost trance-like state of attention. Accept your bonus with good grace! An altered state without a so-called induction.)

COLLAPSING: COMPLETED

At this point you have completed the major work for basic anchoring. You have "polarized," (that is, separated) and established two distinct states in the individual: a + anchor and a – anchor. Next is Anchors Away, which enables the individual to substantially reduce his painful response—in our example, the feelings of depression when alone. Anchors Away is accomplished by simply pressing on the + (left knee) anchor and – (right knee) anchor simultaneously, and holding both until the individual "neutrals" out.

"Neutrals" out simply means that, when you first touch both anchors, the individual will look confused, often spaced-out, with either staring or darting eyes. After a few seconds, the confused, spaced-out look will disappear and the individual will look…well…neutral.

Next, you test your work by touching the – anchor and waiting. If the individual remains neutral—that is, does not go back to the "depressed" state when you touch the anchor—you have then accomplished your basic anchor away or anchor collapse. If the individual collapses back into the – anchor, reinstall a new + anchor and repeat until the – anchor fails to elicit any negative response. My experience, both personally and by having observed several hundred people at my training seminars, leads me to conclude that in only about 20% of the cases will you need to reinstall a second or third + anchor in order to collapse the – anchor.

COLLAPSING: SUBTLETIES

Before we move onto the next step of anchors away, I would like to offer some subtleties for you to be aware of. If the individual's negative state—e.g., depression—is extreme, you may need to establish a somewhat equally powerful + anchor—that is, a powerful + experience—or two, or three + anchors; or you may need to collapse and reinstall a new + anchor, recollapse both anchors, and repeat that procedure until the –

anchor is neutralized. Next, please be aware that not all people will respond in the same way. Some people will respond with full facial and body expression, while others may only clench their jaw or smile slightly. It doesn't matter as long as you can see the change. Some individuals smile immediately when their + anchor is touched, while others may take 10 to 15 seconds to respond. Always give the individual time to respond and watch for *their* way of responding, not your version of how they should respond. You may find the following examples helpful.

At one training seminar, a participant took me aside and told me, "It" wasn't working. Further he told me that, at first, he was doubtful about the whole procedure, yet he had observed it working with other people. I went with him to his practice group, and asked him to repeat the procedure while I watched what he did. After he repeated the procedure he said, "See! It's not working. He doesn't respond at all!" I pressed the + anchor (in this case the subject's right shoulder) and said, "You like that feeling don't you?" The subject nodded very slightly and I then pressed the − anchor (left shoulder) and said, "That's uncomfortable, isn't it?" He nodded again. I then pressed both and, after a few moments, I said, "That's much better, isn't it?" The subject smiled and said "Yes."

The man who had called me aside looked stunned. I pointed out that when he himself pressed the subject's + anchor, the subject took a slow deep breath and looked straight ahead, while, when he pressed the − anchor, the subject stopped breathing for several moments and his lips pressed tightly together. In short, the response was there, but he wasn't watching. In most cases, the responses will be obvious, but be a boy or girl scout: be prepared for the unusual.

At another seminar, a woman told me she couldn't get her subject to respond to a + anchor, but only a − anchor, and that the subject insisted he couldn't get a good feeling. I happened to know that he had just completed a divorce and, according to him, had lost everything. I walked over and said, "John, how would you like to find out that you just came into $250,000 after taxes?" He looked up, smiled and said, "Would I!?" At that point, I squeezed his arm and said cheerfully, "I knew you could remember how to feel good." I asked the woman to complete the exercise and it went without a hitch. In short, be creative. Treat each person as an individual. If you don't get the desired outcome the first time, use a different approach.

Last, but not least, always test the – anchor after you have pressed both to make sure it is collapsed, and only then ask the subject to think about what was making him/her "depressed" and to tell you what is different. The general responses will be: "It seems different" or "It's farther away," or "It seems less important," etc. The reason for not asking until the last is that there are times when the individual is so far behind their unconscious process, that they don't realize the change until you have tested and "shown" them.

BUILDING A NEW RESPONSE

Where the individual's problem is continually being triggered by a real world condition, you must help them to have a new resource for that situation. This will help prevent the "re-triggering" of the old – anchor. There are several ways to accomplish this, but I am going to give you one general way and trust you to develop some others. In our example of the depressed patient, I would ask him to remember some accomplishment or experience in his life that he was pleased with, or even better, proud of. Once he has acknowledged one, I would use systems to anchor that experience: "When you bowled that 250 game, how did you feel?" "How do you think you looked when you were feeling...?" How does your voice sound when you're feeling...?"

At each response, I press gently on the anchor point (which can be wherever you want and good sense dictates). After pressing the anchor for the kinesthetic response, the visual response, and/or the auditory response, I proceed as follows: "Now, I want you to see yourself alone, but this time I want you to experience a change in the way you feel [here I press the + anchor] and see yourself looking good as you feel a certain strong feeling." (Still holding the + anchor) "Now, let's take another situation where you are alone and again notice a growing feeling of strength" (again holding the + anchor). "Next, I want you to see yourself [holding + anchor] in one of those alone situations, but see yourself looking comfortable and feeling comfortable and nod your head when you have accomplished that."

Lastly, stop pressing the + anchor and ask the subject to think about one of those situations that "in the past" caused those "old" feelings, and to see what happens now. I observe to "see" that they remain calm and comfortable. If so, it's time to call it a day. If not, I go and find another positive experience, preferably one that matches the problem situation: e.g., "Can you remember a time you were working on a project alone, and you felt relieved no one was disturbing you?" I repeat the last described anchor experience until the individual evidences comfort while "seeing" the problem area.

ANCHORING ANCHORS

By this time, I trust that you are anchored into the importance of anchoring. Since words, visual stimuli, kinesthetic experience, olfactory and gustatory experience can be, and are, all anchors, then each one of us has unlimited anchors. Why not use what we all are expert at in the first place: Anchoring others! If you will now consider all problems as a form of anchoring, then a hair of the dog may be the most effective way of helping your patients and clients.

The fact that many individuals will "insist" on entering into hypnosis as you utilize anchoring is just something you will have to accept and if, when you collapse an anchor, you ask the individual to close their eyes and they do so, I hope you won't take it personally when they drift off to that "other" state.

XVII
Confessions Of A Hypnotist

Now that I have your attention (I hope), I have a confession to make. At times throughout this book, I have referred to the section on Therapeutic Applications, but there will be no such section. Before you hang me in effigy, read on. Throughout this work, my co-author, Ms. Steele, continued to push, shove and cajole me into clarifying techniques, various approaches, and to give examples which would make sense to you, the reader.

In order to do so, actual cases and therapeutic examples have been used in almost every Chapter. Therefore, you have already read Therapeutic Applications: one part here, one part there, and a little everywhere. Instead of a so-called Therapeutic Applications chapter, I will present several case examples in which the techniques you have learned were either the sole methods, or nearly the sole methods, used. In addition, a few points that have not yet been covered will be in this Chapter. I know you will find the examples given to be useful and valuable in your process of integrating what you have learned.

CASE 12:

Patient is a 45-year-old woman whose presenting problem is phobic fear of flying. (Actually, there is no such thing as a phobic fear of flying. There is a phobic fear of crashing! Think about it.) History: Patient reported that her flying phobia was of 22 years duration, but that she had "always" been leery of flying. As a child, her father had often made comments about the danger of flying and that "sooner or later flying will kill you. It's only a matter of time." In spite of her father's "helpfulness," she had been able to fly, though with a good deal of anxiety. Her phobic response dated from the time (22 years earlier) when a plane she was on lost an engine and had to make an emergency landing. That incident became the trigger for her phobia, or an anchor response.

About one year prior to seeing me, she had attempted to fly to New York after taking Valium and several drinks. However, as soon as she got on the plane, she "freaked out" and had to be let off the airplane. Due to business circumstances, it had now become very important for her to be able to fly.

After she had seated herself in my office, I asked her to tell me about her problem. She immediately looked up to her right (visual). At this point (I could not tell if she was making future or constructive pictures, or if she was left-handed or cross-brained and, therefore, having past visual recall), her hands grasped the arms of the chair, tightened, and she held her breath. Then, in a tight voice, she said, "I am terrified of flying, and I don't think anything can help." At this point, I knew the source of her response: she, upon thinking, speaking or hearing about flying (which would be the trigger) made visual images and responded to those "pictures" with physical feelings and emotions that matched her pictures.

While she continued looking up right and stayed tight, I reached over and squeezed her left wrist and said, "That's a bad feeling, isn't it?" (Installing the – anchor.) She nodded. I then asked her who her favorite grade school teacher was. This was done to both break her pattern and to discover where she would look for past recall. Her eyes went up left and she relaxed substantially. I now knew that her "phobia" response was from constructing future pictures, probably of a plane crashing, and then responding kinesthetically.

After several minutes of making disjointed small talk, jumping from one subject to another (to continue interrupting her pattern and keep her away from her "phobic response"), I asked her what she really liked to do, and did well. She looked up left, smiled, looked down left (auditory), smiled, her face and body relaxed, and she said, "Golf. I really love golf!" I asked her what about golf *sounded* best (remember her auditory eye movement). She said the crisp sound of a well-hit ball; with that, she smiled and her whole body relaxed. I touched her left knee (installing + anchor) and said, "That's a feeling you really enjoy." Next, I asked her to remember a time she played an outstanding round of golf or made a really great shot. (Eyes up left (V) down left (A) and to a big smile while I pressed her left knee again and her left forearm, installing a second + anchor.)

TESTING THE WORK

At this juncture, we have accomplished the following: Discovered the internal source of her problem; her − anchor; her system for pleasant memories; installed the − anchor and two + anchors. All of this was accomplished within 15 minutes from the time she first sat down. Next came testing the work.

I reached over, squeezed her left wrist and said, "Your fear of flying really concerns you, doesn't it?" Immediately her eyes went up right, body tight, etc. Before she could say anything, I let go of her wrist, touched her left knee and said, "But you also know how to feel good." She relaxed, eyes flickered briefly up left, down left, and then she looked at me, smiled, and made some comment on how fast her feelings changed. I repeated the test again, mainly to "show" her, on a non-verbal, unconscious level, how much control she really had over her feelings. My next step was to touch her left knee and squeeze her left wrist at the same time, thereby collapsing the anchors. After she "neutralized," I asked her to think about flying. She looked straight ahead (indicating an unconscious change or restructure), evidenced some tension, and said; "It still upsets me, but it's not nearly so bad."

RESTRUCTURING

I then explained to her how she was able to respond to her pictures, and I was going to help her have a chance to separate her feelings from her pictures (This is one example of the importance of getting people to float out the picture as referred to in Chapter XVI, "Anchors Away.") I asked her to see herself on a roller coaster, and to feel what happened. She responded with observable body sensations. I then asked her to see herself in the roller coaster as if it were someone else, while she silently named her present feelings of sitting in the chair. She was surprised at the difference in her physical response. I now touched her second + anchor (left forearm) and said, "You remember how to feel good, don't you?" As she responded to the + anchor, I instructed her to hold onto the good feeling while she saw herself flying with comfort. We repeated this 4 or 5 times. I then removed my touch and asked her to think about flying. She looked straight ahead, then down left, then straight ahead again (compare that with her initial eye pattern response), and said, "Well, it's not my favorite experience, but I can handle it; it doesn't seem to bother me very much."

The rest of the session was taken up with teaching her Calm Conditioning. (See Chapter XV, "Weighing Anchors.") She was instructed to practice seeing herself flying and, at the first sign of discomfort, to switch to her calm place. She was asked to return the following week so that we could check her work. When she returned, she told me that a strange thing had happened. After two days of practicing calm conditioning, she couldn't concentrate on flying; that every time she tried to see herself flying, her mind would wander and she would find herself remembering pleasant past situations. She also told me that she had made reservations to make a business trip and would send me a postcard. One week later, I got the postcard. It said, "It's still not my favorite activity, but it's better than going to the dentist."

CASE 13:

Patient was a 57-year-old male hospitalized with terminal cancer which had metastasized through areas of his skeletal system. He was in intensive care and, in spite of four to five injections of morphine daily along with oral pain medications, he was suffering intractable pain, insomnia and extreme agitation. His physician asked me to see him about pain control as well as reduction of the patient's agitated state.

When first seen, the patient was complaining in a very harsh tone about his pain. He was thrashing in the bed, and generally being verbally hostile to everyone. (Which, given his circumstances, was to a degree understandable) I noticed that his room contained a portable stereo, a small radio and a small tape recorder. Based on the way he was using his voice (complaining, harsh tone, using many words), and the equipment I had observed, it would be a good guess to assume that he was highly auditory. Since his cancer was causing him pain (throwing him into nearly constant kinesthetic), I knew I needed to get him back to, and then anchor him into, auditory with his visual as a backup system.

UTILIZING SYSTEMS

After introducing myself and gathering some information about his hobbies (he loved *listening* to music), as well as some areas he felt competent in (one of which was working with wood), I was ready to proceed. I asked him if he would mind doing me a favor. (This is a ploy designed to elicit a desire to help me and thereby begin taking an individual's mind off their problem.) I then asked him to close his eyes and listen to what his pain sounded like. He stared at me in disbelief, and I acknowledged that it was a strange request, but I really needed him to do me that favor.

With that, he closed his eyes and appeared to be concentrating. Almost immediately, his breathing deepened and he became much more still (still moving but without the almost wild thrashing). After a minute or so, he opened his eyes and said, "It's like a terrible grinding sound." I asked him to close his eyes again and listen to the grinding sound to discover how much it might sound like one of his woodworking grinders or drills. In a few moments he nodded slowly.

I next asked him to get a clear picture of the tool that most reminded him of the sound and to nod when he had it—which he did within a few seconds. I then asked him to "see" that tool or machine across the room in his mind's eye, and to speed it up as fast as he could. Within several seconds, he nodded again. I then instructed him to "see" the tool or machine slowing down, little by little, until it had stopped.

As he nodded this time, I gently squeezed his left shoulder and simply said, "That's good; you're really helping." (Intentionally not specifying who or what he was helping.) At this point, his transformation was remarkable. He was no longer moving around, his breathing was very deep and slow, his face was relaxed, and his color had changed.

The next step in my procedure was to help him remember how he could forget annoyances. This was done by talking slowly and in a low tone (remember his auditory) about working on wood and how you could turn on loud equipment such as a grinder and not even notice the noise; that he became so deeply involved in what he was making, that he forgot the noise! He slowly nodded. Since we had already established that his pain sounded like grinding, I was betting that he would make the connection between forgetting the sound and forgetting the pain.

During this monologue, I continued the gentle squeeze on his left shoulder. I then began to discuss listening to music, and how easy it was to lose track of time and place when you're really engrossed; and how you could almost float away from everything while listening to music. He nodded slowly again. (By this time he was so much into "that state" that he didn't respond to nurses and other staff coming into the room.)

I ended this first session by telling him that I didn't know just what sounds around him were going to remind him of floating away. While I continued to gently squeeze his shoulder, I began to mention common hospital sounds that might do that—in short, anchoring him into "floating" away as a result of hearing the hospital sounds.

RESULTS

When I returned to see him two days later, he had been transferred from intensive care to the observation unit as a result of the changes he had evidenced. He had begun sleeping through the night; he was eating; and his attitude had undergone a remarkable change for the better. In addition, he had had only one shot each of the two days, and had substantially reduced his intake of other drugs.

In this second session, I "taught" him how to "see" and/or "hear" his pain so that he could begin to take more responsibility for his treatment, and then I basically repeated the steps of his first session. By the third session, which was six days after I first saw him, he had not required any shots and only two Valiums (one each on two different nights) to "help me sleep." The day after his third session, he was discharged from the hospital.

Several weeks later, I received a very nice letter from his wife. In it she stated that he was still almost totally pain free, with occasional Valium use at bedtime; that he was cheerful and spent a lot of time in his workshop finishing (wood) projects that he had started over the years. (We could say he was reinforcing his hypnotic suggestion by actual work.)

CASE 14:

A 25-year-old, newly-married woman was referred by her physician for what he termed "frigidity." Her history indicated, however, that she was touch phobic. She told me that if she got stoned enough she could have sex and respond, but, when sober, she became almost physically sick from being touched in any "sexual" way. She also stated that she did not like to be touched in any way by anyone.

I positioned myself in such a way that my right foot was close to her left foot, while being careful to maintain a "discreet" distance from her. I then proceeded to tell her stories, ask questions and make general comments to elicit in her a smile or laughter. Each time she laughed or smiled, I pressed my foot against hers very gently. I asked her about any pleasant vacations she had been on. As she responded with a smile, I would press my foot against hers again.

When telling me about her problem, she would look up (V past) while tensing up in the chair, (K manifestation). However, while discussing pleasant experiences, she would look up left (V past) down left (A), look at me (V present) and smile (K present). This procedure continued for about 20 minutes, at which point I moved my body in closer to her. After some joke or story she laughed heartily and, as she did so, I reached over and touched her left wrist and said, "Laughter looks good on you; I bet it feels even better." She nodded and said, "It sure does." I continued to find ways to elicit smiles or laughter and continued to touch her left wrist until finally I just left my hand resting on hers and said, "Well, it appears you can see yourself [keeping it visual] learning to have good feelings while being touched." She looked down at my hand on her wrist, looked puzzled, looked up and said, "Well, I'll be damned!"

At the end of her first session, I walked her out into the lobby, where several people were seated. I told her I would see her next week, and with that, she turned and gave me almost a bear hug and said, "God, I feel great!" Her action put *me* into hypnosis, but it also indicated how far she had come in one session.

For her second session, the procedure was a basic anchor collapse: Inserting several + anchors and then eliciting her bad feelings at being touched (which at this point weren't very bad at all), installing the − anchor, and then collapsing. Lastly, she was taught calm conditioning, and was instructed to practice seeing herself being intimate with her husband while either holding on to the calm feeling, or, if she experienced anxiety, to switch to her calm place. A follow-up several months later revealed that she not only was over her "frigidity" but she had no problem with touching.

COMMENT

Over the years I have evolved a theory about so-called touch phobia, and find the condition simple to ameliorate. First, I believe that this condition arises because a person's history is one of almost never being touched as a child except when they were hurt or were being punished. In short, they have been anchored into associating pain with touch. Secondly, based on this belief, the procedure—as outlined in this case—collapses the old anchor and installs a new association or anchor: pleasurable feelings and touch. At my training seminars, I explain this to the participants and ask them to check it out and keep me informed. From the results, I must conclude that the theory is correct or the techniques produce the results in spite of my theory.

CASE 15:

This will be a brief case as reported by a former seminar participant. Her client was a man in his mid-forties with a presenting problem of severe headaches resulting from almost constant jaw clenching. Her approach was to continue to anchor collapse: that is, she would ask the man to remember something pleasant, install a + anchor and then ask him to clench his jaw while she fired off the + anchor. She repeated this procedure over and over during a one hour session: installing a + anchor, asking him to clench, firing the + anchor. Her client reported the following week that every time he started to clench his teeth, something clicked and he would find himself remembering something *pleasant* and his jaw would relax. He also reported that he had only two headaches in the whole week.

She simply repeated her procedure for the second session, and her client reported a complete absence of headaches. A follow-up call one month later (his calling her at her request), indicated that he was still symptom free and, in addition, that he was sleeping better and had much more energy.

In outlining her case to me, she pointed out that when her client was clenching his jaw, he was also looking down left. This would indicate a hear/feel loop: that is, talking to himself (A) and responding with jaw clenching (K). However, when discussing pleasant things, he looked up left, then right, then straight ahead and would smile (V past, visual future, visual present with kinesthetic response). After the first session, two unconscious changes were noted: When he would look down left (A) and just as he would start to clench (K), he would immediately look up left (V past) and then straight ahead with no jaw clenching or he would look down left (A) and pull his head up (K) and look straight ahead (V present).

From the above cases, you may conclude that it sounds too easy. Well, you can lead a camel to water, but you can't make it fly a 747! At training seminars, I have observed someone do a procedure beautifully, get observable results, have the subject verify it, and yet they complain there must be more to it. By the time they are done hypnotizing themselves into believing that it must be harder than that, or that there's got to be a catch, they have made it difficult or impossible for themselves. To me, that's crazy. But, if everyone were rational and made sense, I would have to find another way to make a living.

XVIII

Ramblings

I don't know about you, the reader, but writing this last Chapter elicits mixed feelings within me. I am, at the same time, relieved and glad that the damned thing is finished, and yet strangely sad. Ms. Steele and myself have put lots of hours, effort, research and the proverbial blood, sweat and tears into this work. As you have probably surmised by now, I am not, nor will I ever be an academician, and, therefore, I found writing about Unconscious Restructuring®, hypnosis, and my approach to be far more difficult than the actual doing.

Since you are reading this part, I can assume you were stubborn enough, curious enough, and perverse enough to have read all that has preceded. With those qualities, I know you will be successful in utilizing what...*you have learned!* I also hope you will permit me to ramble, and even if you don't, it's my intention to do so.

While growing up as a hypnotist, I always resented those books in which it was implied 1) that the author never "missed," and, 2) that the successes were always instantaneous—while the method of producing the "miracle" was somehow, strangely missing. Two pages might be devoted to detailing the seriousness and difficulty of the problem, while the methodology would be reduced to, "After three [or 2 or 1 or 4] sessions in which hypnosis was induced and strong suggestion given, the patient was forever happy (or?).

That always reminded me of fairy tales in which the prince and princess rode off to live happily ever after...but no one told you about the next day. To put it another way, I always had the feeling I either had missed something (the method) or was just plain dumb (perhaps I should have *known* the method). I sincerely hope I have avoided those two situations in this work. First, I have made every effort to give you, in detail, the method, words and approach used with each individual. Secondly, I want to make it clear that at times I fail miserably, and fall flat on my...(fill in). That is not a comment on Unconscious Restructuring®, but rather on my failure to have used the approach wisely; or to have failed in being observant enough; or times I have allowed myself to become impatient from overwork or too few vacations; or from being too sloppy. However, I believe I have learned and improved my method more from the so-called failures than from the successes.

REVIEW: BELIEF SYSTEMS

Now that I have "that" out of the way, I would like to ramble about the subject of the book itself. When an individual presents him/herself at your office, I believe that they are saying in effect: "My belief system is preventing me from exercising new choices." If their belief system was effective in the problem area, they would have solved the problem and would not need you. If you accept their belief system as being true in reality, then you not only have been hypnotized by them, you also run the risk of perpetuating and becoming part of that problem.

Therefore, your first task is to help them expand and/or challenge the belief system that is keeping them stuck. Next, you must consider that a form of self-hypnosis is keeping their belief system going. That individual is somehow hallucinating to stay stuck; for example: "not seeing" times they have been "liked" while finding evidence they are disliked—which in traditional hypnotist circles would be recognized as positive and negative hallucinations. When you argue with a person who is "seeing" or "not seeing" an hypnotic hallucination, they entrench and become more "positive" of what they "see" or "don't see." So, whether you use hypnosis formally or not, I believe you must be aware of the hypnotic factor involved in maintaining the individual's painful state. You either use this awareness, or end up being a hypnotic subject yourself.

REVIEW: SYSTEMS

I further contend that a person who is functioning well, either in all areas or some area, is utilizing all systems (V—K—A) in a synergistic manner, while the more that individual relies on one system to the exclusion of one or more of the other systems, the less choice they have available, and the more stuck and in pain they become. Within every system is stored experiences, knowledge and the skills that can lead to new choices, behaviors and responses. If a person "sees" himself failing, you may help them to remember a time they "felt" successful, and that feeling may help them build a picture of being successful. The new picture will itself lead to a challenge of the old belief system. If an individual has always been "told" they shouldn't speak up, you can help them recall visually times they saw people speak up; that visual memory can help them change their belief that they shouldn't speak up. It is therefore incumbent upon the therapist to help the individual expand and balance his systems.

Where therapists continue to use the same system as the individual, and accept the individual's belief system, then the client/patient is doing an exquisite job of causing the therapist to "see" or "hear" or "feel" the same way the patient does. Of course, we must keep in mind there's no such thing as hypnosis. By recognizing the individual's limited use of systems and their self-defeating belief systems, the therapist immediately becomes equipped with a multitude of choices as to how to proceed to help the individual.

If someone is lost in the wilderness, it is foolish to build a base station and wait for them to find you. You have to go where they are and lead them out. To sum up the point, we could say that the individual has been hypnotized into believing that certain things are a certain way and will *always* be that way. Through circumstances, the individual, in his problem area at least, begins to develop reliance on a particular system—whether kinesthetic, visual or auditory—for attempting to deal with the problem. Through these processes, the person begins to "distort" reality, and by so doing, they continue to "see," "hear" and "feel" the same thing over and over. In effect, they keep themselves in a hypnotic state during which their belief system takes precedence over so-called "consensual" reality. I believe that if you use the same mechanism that produces the problem—hypnosis—you can help them to quickly break patterns, develop new skills and respond with new choices. If a person already is skilled at using a hammer, help them to use the hammer differently while showing them how to use a screwdriver. Don't demand they fly a plane instead. (You will have to think about that.)

REVIEW: PATTERN INTERRUPTION

I would like you to consider that human beings are energy conserving (some would say lazy). We build machines to do our work, and then machines to run our machines, and then use computers to supervise. This is said to point out that people naturally streamline their behavior into patterns: patterns that are repetitive and energy conserving. Where these patterns are effective and lead to successful outcomes, we have a good system. However, where an individual continues to repeat painful patterns—e.g., becomes "depressed" every weekend, or when they are alone, etc.—it then becomes an "absolute must" to interrupt those (painful) patterns and help them to develop more effective patterns of response.

As we pointed out earlier, where a pattern is interrupted, an individual will often go into a hypnotic state. This gives you a golden opportunity to help them to install a new and more efficacious response. Since we all have long and successful histories of learning, unlearning and changing patterns, it is already built into the system to change patterns. However, no human being develops a pattern unless, at some point in their history, that pattern "seemed" necessary. That is not to say it *was* necessary, only that it *seemed* so. Therefore, part of the individual's belief system is that the pattern is *needed*. Helping them to break patterns also may help them to challenge belief systems without ever discussing belief systems.

I've said it before, and I want to say it again: "Therapy, any therapy, succeeds where, by hook or by crook, on purpose or by accident, the therapist has helped the individual to break a pattern and substitute a new pattern in its place."

After working with hundreds of individuals in my clinical practice and giving dozens of training seminars, I have become convinced of the following: People respond in their problem areas (and, perhaps, in their successful areas) as an hypnotic subject would to so-called post-hypnotic suggestion. They will tell you that, "Every time s/he looks or talks or...that way, I get depressed or angry or [fill in]," or "Every time I think of...I become..." If you compare these phenomena and the individual's consistency of response with the literature on post-hypnotic suggestion, I believe that you, too, will be struck by the similarity. If you accept this thesis, then it stands to reason that hypnotic techniques are the antidote to hypnotically produced and continued problems and limitations.

REVIEW: ANCHORING

In this work, two chapters were devoted to the subject of anchoring. I would like you to consider anchoring as a different way of producing post-hypnotic suggestion. Or, you may want to consider post-hypnotic suggestion as a different way of producing anchors. I will leave that up to you. Either way, you can have a powerful understanding of what produces and continues limitations and problems.

In my office, I have imitated a tone of voice or a facial expression that a person says upsets them; I have observed them cry, get angry and, in one case, attempt to "punch me out." It was as if they were "automatons," responding without choice or awareness. Helping them to "collapse" those anchors helped them to have choices.

Since I believe that no one *wants* to suffer, helping them to have choice leads them to find more satisfying and pleasurable ways of dealing with the world. If you are not aware of anchors (post-hypnotic suggestions), you run the risk of reinforcing them and triggering them. That's OK if you have a reason and a goal and intend to break the pattern and collapse the painful response.

Since, with hypnotic techniques such as anchoring, you can cause an individual to respond to a pencil with anxiety or to a facial expression with happiness, it would seem very important for you to stop trying to make sense out of nonsense. If logic and left-hemispheric thought could have resolved the problems, the problems would have been resolved. Instead, if you will consider all presenting problems as some form of anchor or anchors produced by a form of hypnosis, your tasks will be simplified. All you will need to do is develop the techniques to help the person respond in more useful ways. This will be accomplished by recognizing (not analyzing) their belief system; which system (V—K—A) they need to develop; how to break the pattern; and what anchors (post-hypnotic suggestion) you need to neutralize; and what new patterns you need to install and reinforce.

Last, but not least, I do not believe that any book, even (or perhaps moreso) this one, can replace getting in there and trying new things. So many of us are afraid that we might make a mistake, or our patient/client might not like us. In truth, we're not getting paid to be liked, and our clients don't know what is going to work and what is not. I invite you, no I implore you, to attempt what you have read and more. Each day do something unexpected in your practice (and your life); change chairs, change clothes, change!! Use a new technique. You will probably become more effective. I know it will keep you challenged, excited and happier and, please remember, there's no such thing as hypnosis.

Epilogue

Hypnotists: Charlatans. Evildoers. Controllers of men.
Mesmer. Svengali. Rasputin. Dracula. THE DEVIL HIMSELF.
Do you see him? Do you hear his silken voices telling you to do his
bidding? You know you must not look; if you do you are lost; lost
forever. You cannot help yourself. You try to pull away. But his eyes
lock with yours. You can hear nothing but his voice. You are helpless.
And your soul is his. Forever.

Or: Stage magic. Cheap entertainment. Fraud.
As you sit comfortably in your seat, you watch from the safety of
distance. The Great Fraudini, Hypnotist Extraordinaire, has his helpless
victim on stage, ready for the first humiliation. "Bark like a dog," he
says, and the poor schnook gets down on all fours and barks. "Your seat
is getting hot," he suggests, and the fool jumps through the roof and you
laugh. "You're naked," Fraudini intones and you can almost feel his
victim's embarrassment as he tries to cover his nudity. And, suddenly,
you realize that you feel uncomfortable, too.
Empathy, you call it. After all, it's just a performance and the
"Victim" is probably just going along with the gag. And, even if it isn't
just a set-up, it must be that Fraudini picked a particularly "suggestible"
subject—weak-minded, slow-witted and dull. Not like you, of course. It
could never work on you.
It might occur to you...*NOW*...that as you felt your own discomfort,
Fraudini was hypnotizing you as much as his subject. Maybe you went
into your own experience and remembered a time when you were
uncomfortable and em-bare-assed. Maybe you had a picture of that time
and heard the voice of that person and remembered.

These are the symbols of hypnotism, of "mesmerism" as it was once
called. Before I met Dr. Heller I was "hypnotised" by these symbols. I
"knew" what hypnosis was all about. I said to myself, "I'm not some

backwoods hick. I have an education. I'm knowledgeable and aware." So I thought I knew what I was talking about. But symbols and cues and triggers and anchors are powerful things.

As you know by now, hypnosis, as practiced by men like Milton Erickson and Steve Heller, has nothing to do with spinning wheels and suggestions of "deeper and deeper." (While we're on the subject of "deeper," Steve liked to remind us that Ph.D. is simply an abbreviation for "Piled Higher and Deeper." And he loved multiple meanings. Even his license plate read "HYP PHD." And consider the name he gave his methodology: "Unconscious Restructuring®.")

Well, it's taken a long time, but finally, now, hypnosis is becoming reputable. Not just as a trick, not even just as a limited treatment modality for smoking or stress reduction or weight control, but as a powerful mechanism for real change. Real Change. The scientific research is there. Change at the level of the limbic system. (See, for example, *The Psychobiology of Mind-Body Healing: New Concepts of Therapeutic Hypnosis* by Ernest L. Rossi, Ph.D., W.W. Norton Co., Inc., New York, 1986.) Steve's methods work. Just by "telling stories."

Now that you have read this book you can see clearly that it is no accident that Dr. Steven Heller was known as The Wizard. But, maybe, you still don't believe in hypnosis. I know I didn't. And, after reading this book, I still don't.

On October 24, 1997, Steve Heller, The Wizard, left us. Though his work and his legacy endures, his presence, his sense of humor, and his enormous energy are gone. As one of his many friends I miss him.

Nicholas Tharcher
March 2001

Bibliography

Aitchison, Jean. *The Articulate Mammal: An Introduction to Psycholinguistics.* New York, Universe Books, 1976.

Aziz, Barbara. "Second Look: Maps and the Mind." *Human Nature,* 1979, Vol. 2, Number 1, 34.

Bandler, R., & Grinder, J. *The Structure of Magic I.* Palo Alto, CA, Science and Behavior Books, Inc., 1975.

Bandler, R., & Grinder, J. *The Structure of Magic II.* Palo Alto, CA, Science and Behavior Books, 1976.

Buzan, T., & Dizon, T. *The Evolving Brain.* N.Y., Chicago, San Francisco, Dallas, Holt, Rinehart & Winston.

Edwards, Betty. *Drawing on the Right Side of the Brain: A Course in Enhancing Creativity and Artistic Confidence.* Tarcher/St. Martins Press, 1979.

Erickson, M.H., Rossi, E.L., & Rossi, S.I., *Hypnotic Realities: The Induction of Clinical Hypnosis and Forms of Indirect Suggestion.* New York, Irvington Publishers, 1976.

Erickson, M.H. & Rossi, E.L. *Hypnotherapy: An Exploratory Casebook.* Irvington Publishers, New York, 1979.

Gazzaneza, M.S. *The Split Brain in Man.* Progress in Psychobiology: Readings from *Scientific American,* 1967, August, 372. San Francisco, W.F. Freeman & Co.

Haley, J. (Ed.) *Advanced Techniques of Hypnosis and Therapy: Selected Papers of Milton H. Erickson.* New York, Grune and Stratton, 1967.

Hamilton, Max. *Psychosomatics.* New York, John Wiley & Sons, Inc., 1955.

Homer, A. & Buhler, C. *Existential and Humanistic Psychology: A Hope for the Future in Philosophy, Psychotherapy and Research.* International Psychiatry Clinics, 1969, 6 (3), 55–73.

Ittelson, W.H. & Kilpatrick, F.P. *Experiments in Perception. The Nature of Human Consciousness: A Book of Readings.* Ornstein, R. (Ed.) San Francisco, W.H. Freeman & Co., 1973.

Kroger, Wm. S. *Clinical and Experimental Hypnosis in Medicine, Dentistry, and Psychology.* Philadelphia, Lippincott, 1963.

Kroger, Wm. S. & Felzler, Wm. D. *Hypnosis and Behavior Modification: Imagery Conditioning.* Philadelphia, Lippincott, 1976.

Luria, A.R. *The Working Brain.* New York, Basic Books, Inc., 1973.

Maslow, A.H. *The Farther Reaches of Human Nature.* New York, Viking Press, 1971.

Miller, G.A., Galanter, E., and Pribrim, K.H. *Plans and the Structure of Behavior.* New York, Chicago, San Francisco, Dallas. Holt, Reinhart and Winston, Inc., 1960.

Ornstein, R.E. *The Psychology of Consciousness.* San Francisco, W.H. Freeman and Co., 1972.

Penfield, W. & Roberts, L. *Speech and Brain Mechanisms.* Princeton, N.J., Princeton University Press, 1959.

Salter, A. *Conditioned Reflex Therapy: The direct approach to the reconstruction of personality.* New York, Creative Age Press, 1949.

Shevrin, H. & Dickman, S. "The Psychological Unconscious: A necessary assumption for all Psychological Theory?" *American Psychologist,* 1980, Vol. 35, Number 5, 421–434.

Smokler & Shevrin. *Archives of Psychiatry,* 36: 949–954. Reported in *Brain Mind Bulletin,* Jan. 7, 1980, Vol. 5, Number 4.

Watzlawick, P. *The Language of Change.* New York, Basic Books, Inc., 1978.

Wolberg, L.R. *Hypnoanalysis.* New York, Grune and Stratton, Inc., 1964.

Wolman, B. *Dictionary of Behavioral Science.* New York, Van Nustrand Reinhold Co., 1973.

Young, J.Z. *Program of the Brain,* Oxford, Oxford University Press, 1978.

About The Author

Steven Heller, Ph.D., founder and director of The Heller Institute, had a clinical hypnosis practice since 1969. He was widely in demand as a lecturer and trainer of the Ericksonian method, as well as his own method, Unconscious Restructuring®. Through his seminar program, Clinical Hypnosis: Innovative Techniques® Dr. Heller was one of the first individuals to present what was to become known as "Ericksonian hypnotherapy." This program was presented throughout the country for several years. As a result he became known as the "trainer of the trainers," and was given the name "The Wizard."

In addition to his private practice, Dr. Heller trained members of the helping professions, and conducted in-house training programs for hospital staffs, universities, medical, dental and psychological associations. He was a guest on several radio and television programs. Dr. Heller utilized his methods for surgical procedures, in which general anesthesia could not be used. One dramatic example was the use of Unconscious Restructuring® as the sole anesthesia during a mastectomy. Not only was the patient free from pain during the procedure, she also required no postoperative medication. She was also discharged 36 hours post surgery.

Dr. Heller received his Ph.D. in clinical psychology from California Western University, where his special area of study was, of course, hypnosis. He was born in Los Angeles in 1939 and died in 1997. He is deeply missed.

New Falcon Publications

Invites You to Visit Our Website:
http://www.newfalcon.com

At the Falcon website you can:

- Browse the online catalog of all of our great titles
- Find out what's available and what's out of stock
- Get special discounts
- Order our titles through our secure online server
- Find products not available anywhere else including:
  – One of a kind and limited availability products
  – Special packages
  – Special pricing
- Get free gifts
- Join our email list for advance notice of New Releases and Special Offers
- Find out about book signings and author events
- Send email to our authors (including the elusive Dr. Christopher Hyatt!)
- Read excerpts of many of our titles
- Find links to our author's websites
- Discover links to other weird and wonderful sites
- And much, much more

Get online today at http://www.newfalcon.com